CONTENTS

CW01507206

OSBORNE REVISE!

ACCA

ACCA F3 Financial Accounting

NOTES

© Osborne Books Limited, 2017.

First edition.

Published by Osborne Books Limited

Unit 2
The Business Centre
Molly Millars Lane
Wokingham
Berkshire RG41 2QZ

Tel 01905 748071

Email books@osbornebooks.co.uk

Website www.osbornebooks.co.uk

Printed and bound in Great Britain.

British Library Cataloguing in Publication Data

A catalogue record for this book is available from the British Library

ISBN 978-1-911198-23-9

HOW TO USE THESE *ACCA Notes*

These *ACCA Notes* have been designed to help you to:

- **Renew** your approach to syllabus areas that might not have been clear first time around. Use them to supplement your learning and to help you to clarify details of the syllabus of which you are unsure. It is easy to look things up using the detailed index and contents page and find quickly the topic you need help with

- **Refresh** topics you have covered before but may have forgotten. If it is a while since you studied a topic which underpins a higher level subject that you now need to study, for example, use them as a refresher tool to remind yourself of what you have already learnt

- **Revise** and make the best use of your time before your examinations. Take advantage of the summarised topics, learning summaries, summary diagrams, key points, definitions and exam tips to support your revision in the critical period leading up to your real exam.

PREPARING FOR THE EXAM

To pass your exam you need an understanding of the syllabus and exam technique is vital. These *ACCA Notes* follow the syllabus with succinct coverage, offering tips on how to get the best results in the exam.

ACCA Notes – ICONS

LEARNING SUMMARY

The 'learning summary' provides details of the key learning objectives of each section of content.

DEFINITION

The 'definition' boxes highlight and explain key terms.

KEY POINT

The 'key point' boxes emphasise key points which are fundamental to your understanding of the syllabus.

Do you understand?

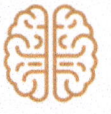

The 'do you understand' boxes contain short form questions which are not necessarily exam style, but which test that you have understood the core syllabus content before you progress onto exam style questions.

PAPER INFORMATION

The aim of ACCA Paper F3, Financial Accounting, FIA Diploma in Accounting and Business, Financial Accounting, is to develop knowledge and understanding of the underlying principles and concepts relating to financial accounting and technical proficiency in the use of double-entry accounting techniques including the preparation of basic financial statements.

SYLLABUS

A   THE CONTEXT AND PURPOSE OF FINANCIAL REPORTING

1   The scope and purpose of, financial statements for external reporting

(a)   Define financial reporting – recording, analysing and summarising financial data.[k] **Ch 1**

(b)   Identify and define types of business entity – sole trader, partnership, limited liability company. [k] **Ch 1**

(c)   Recognise the legal differences between a sole trader, partnership and a limited liability company. [k] **Ch 1**

(d)   Identify the advantages and disadvantages of operating as a limited liability company, sole trader or partnership. [k] **Ch 1**

(e)   Understand the nature, principles and scope of financial reporting.[k] **Ch 1**

2   Users' and stakeholders' needs

(a)   Identify the users of financial statements and state and differentiate between their information needs.[k] **Ch 1**

3   The main elements of financial reports

(a)   Understand and identify the purpose of each of the main financial statements. [k] **Ch 1**

(b)   Define and identify assets, liabilities, equity, revenue and expenses. [k] **Ch 1**

4   The regulatory framework

(a)   Understand the role of the regulatory system including the roles of the IFRS® Foundation (the Foundation), the International Accounting Standards Board (The Board), the IFRS Advisory Council (IFRS AC) and the IFRS Interpretations Committee (IFRIC®).[k] **Ch 2**

(b)   Understand the role of International Financial Reporting Standards (IFRS Standards®).[k] **Ch 2**

5   Duties and responsibilities of those charged with governance

(a)   Explain what is meant by governance specifically in the context of the preparation of financial statements.[k] **Ch 2**

(b)   Describe the duties and responsibilities of directors and other parties covering the preparation of the financial statements.[k] **Ch 2**

B **THE QUALITATIVE CHARACTERISTICS OF FINANCIAL INFORMATION**

1 **The qualitative characteristics of financial information**

(a) Define, understand and apply qualitative characteristics: [k] **Ch 1**

    (i) Relevance

    (ii) Faithful representation

    (iii) Comparability

    (iv) Verifiability

    (v) Timeliness

    (vi) Understandability

(b) Define, understand and apply accounting concepts **Ch 1**

    (i) Materiality

    (ii) Substance over form

    (iii) Going concern

    (iv) Business entity concept

    (v) Accruals

    (vi) Fair presentation

    (vii) Consistency

C THE USE OF DOUBLE ENTRY AND ACCOUNTING SYSTEMS

1 **Double entry bookkeeping principles including the maintenance of accounting records**

(a) Identify and explain the function of the main data sources in an accounting system.[k] **Ch 3**

(b) Outline the contents and purpose of different types of business documentation, including: quotation, sales order, purchase order, goods received note, goods despatched note, invoice, statement, credit note, debit note, remittance advice, receipt.[k] **Ch 3**

(c) Understand and apply the concept of double entry accounting and the duality concept. [k] **Ch 3**

(d) Understand and apply the accounting equation[s]. **Ch 3**

(e) Understand how the accounting system contributes to providing useful accounting information and complies with organisational policies and deadlines. [k] **Ch 1 & 3**

(f) Identify the main types of business transactions, e.g. sales, purchases, payments, receipts. [k] **Ch 3**

2 **Ledger accounts, books of prime entry and journals**

(a) Identify the main types of ledger accounts and books of prime entry, and understand their nature and function. [k] **Ch 3**

(b) Understand and illustrate the uses of journals and the posting of journal entries into ledger accounts. [s] **Ch 4**

(c) Identify correct journals from given narrative. [s]   **Ch 3**

(d) Illustrate how to balance and close a ledger account.[s] **Ch 4**

D RECORDING TRANSACTIONS AND EVENTS

1   Sales and purchases

(a)   Record sale and purchase transactions in ledger accounts.[s] **Ch 4, 11, 12**

(b)   Understand and record sales and purchase returns.[s] **Ch 5**

(c)   Understand the general principles of the operation of a sales tax.[k] **Ch 5**

(d)   Calculate sales tax on transactions and record the consequent accounting entries.[s] **Ch 5**

(e)   Account for discounts allowed and discounts received.[s] **Ch 5**

2   Cash

(a)   Record cash transactions in ledger accounts. [s]   **Ch 4**

(b)   Understand the need for a record of petty cash transactions.[k] **Ch 3, 14**

3   Inventory

(a)   Recognise the need for adjustments for inventory in preparing financial statements.[k] **Ch 6**

(b)   Record opening and closing inventory. [s]   **Ch 6**

(c)   Identify the alternative methods of valuing inventory. [k] **Ch 6**

(d)   Understand and apply the IASB requirements for valuing inventories.[s] **Ch 6**

(e)   Recognise which costs should be included in valuing inventories.[s] **Ch 6**

(f)   Understand the use of continuous and period end inventory records. [k] **Ch 6**

(g)   Calculate the value of closing inventory using FIFO (first in, first out) and AVCO (average cost) – both periodic weighted average and continuous weighted average.[s] **Ch 6**

(h)   Understand the impact of accounting concepts on the valuation of inventory.[k] **Ch 6**

(i)   Identify the impact of inventory valuation methods on profit and on assets.[s] **Ch 6**

4   Tangible non-current assets

(a)   Define non-current assets. [k] **Ch 1 & 7**

(b)   Recognise the difference between current and non-current assets. [k] **Ch 1 & 7**

(c)   Explain the difference between capital and revenue items. [k] **Ch 7**

(d)   Classify expenditure as capital or revenue expenditure.[s] **Ch 7**

(e)   Prepare ledger entries to record the acquisition and disposal of non-current assets.[s] **Ch 7 & 8**

(f)   Calculate and record profits or losses on disposal of non-current assets in the statement of profit or loss, including part exchange transactions. [s] **Ch 8**

(g)   Record the revaluation of a non-current asset in ledger accounts, the statement of profit or loss and other comprehensive income and in the statement of financial position.[s] **Ch 8**

(h)   Calculate the profit or loss on disposal of a revalued asset.[s] **Ch 8**

(i)   Illustrate how non-current asset balances and movements are disclosed in financial statements. [s] **Ch 7 & 8**

(j)   Explain the purpose and function of an asset register. [k] **Ch 7**

5   Depreciation

(a)   Understand and explain the purpose of depreciation. [k] **Ch 7**

(b)   Calculate the charge for depreciation using straight line and reducing balance methods.[s] **Ch 7**

(c)   Identify the circumstances where different methods of depreciation would be appropriate.[k] **Ch 7**

(d)   Illustrate how depreciation expense and accumulated depreciation are recorded in ledger accounts.[s] **Ch 7**

(e)   Calculate depreciation on a revalued non-current asset including the transfer of excess depreciation between the revaluation surplus and retained earnings.[s] **Ch 8**

(f)   Calculate the adjustments to depreciation necessary if changes are made in the estimated useful life and/or residual value of a non-current asset.[s]   (g)   **Ch 7**

(g)   Record depreciation in the statement of profit or loss and statement of financial position.[s] **Ch 7**

6   Intangible non-current assets and amortisation

(a)   Recognise the difference between tangible and intangible non-current assets.[k] **Ch 9**

(b)   Identify types of intangible assets.[k] **Ch 9**

(c)   Identify the definition and treatment of 'research costs' and 'development costs' in accordance with International Financial Reporting Standards. [k] **Ch 9**

(d)   Calculate amounts to be capitalised as development expenditure or to be expensed from given information.[s] **Ch 9**

(e)   Explain the purpose of amortisation.[k] **Ch 9**

(f)   Calculate and account for the charge for amortisation.[s] **Ch 9**

7   Accruals and prepayments

(a)   Understand how the matching concept applies to accruals and prepayments.[k] **Ch 10**

(b)   Identify and calculate the adjustments needed for accruals and prepayments in preparing financial statements.[s] **Ch 10**

(c)   Illustrate the process of adjusting for accruals and prepayments in preparing financial statements.[s] **Ch 10**

(d)   Prepare the journal entries and ledger entries for the creation of an accrual or prepayment.[s] **Ch 10**

(e)   Understand and identify the impact on profit and net assets of accruals and prepayments.[s] **Ch 10**

8   Receivables and payables

(a)   Explain and identify examples of receivables and payables.[k] **11 & 12**

(b)   Identify the benefits and costs of offering credit facilities to customers.[k] **Ch 11**

(c)   Understand the purpose of an aged receivables analysis.[k] **Ch 11**

(d)   Understand the purpose of credit limits.[k] **Ch 11**

(e)   Prepare the bookkeeping entries to write off a irrecoverable debt.[s]

(f)   Record an irrecoverable debt recovered.[s] **Ch 11**

(g)   Identify the impact of irrecoverable debts on the statement of profit or loss and on the statement of financial position.[s] **Ch 11**

(h) Prepare the bookkeeping entries to create and adjust an allowance for receivables.[s] **Ch 11**

(i) Illustrate how to include movements in the allowance for receivables in the statement of profit or loss and how the closing balance of the allowance should appear in the statement of financial position.[s] **Ch 11**

(j) Account for contras between trade receivables and payables.[s] **Ch 14**

(k) Prepare, reconcile and understand the purpose of supplier statements.[s] **Ch 14**

(l) Classify items as current or non-current liabilities in the statement of financial position.[s] **Ch 1**

9   Provisions and contingencies

(a) Understand the definition of 'provision', 'contingent liability' and 'contingent asset'.[k] **Ch 12**

(b) Distinguish between and classify items as provisions, contingent liabilities or contingent assets.[k] **Ch 12**

(c) Identify and illustrate the different methods of accounting for provisions, contingent liabilities and contingent assets.[k] **Ch 12**

(d) Calculate provisions and changes in provisions.[s] **Ch 12**

(e) Account for the movement in provisions.[s] **Ch 12**

(f) Report provisions in the final accounts. [s] **Ch 12**

10   Capital structure and finance costs

(a) Understand the capital structure of a limited liability company including: [k] **Ch 13**

(i) ordinary shares

(ii) preference shares (redeemable and irredeemable)

(iii) loan notes.

(b) Record movements in the share capital and share premium accounts.[s] **Ch 13**

(c) Identify and record the other reserves which may appear in the company statement of financial position.[s] **Ch 13**

(d) Define a bonus (capitalisation) issue and its advantages and disadvantages.[k] **Ch 13**

(e) Define a rights issue and its advantages and disadvantages.[k]

(f) Record and show the effects of a bonus (capitalisation) issue in the statement of financial position.[s] **Ch 13**

(g) Record and show the effects of a rights issue in the statement of financial position.[s] **Ch 13**

(h) Record dividends in ledger accounts and the financial statements.[s] **Ch 13**

(i) Calculate and record finance costs in ledger accounts and the financial statements.[s] **Ch 13**

(j) Identify the components of the statement of changes in equity.[k] **Ch 16**

E PREPARING A TRIAL BALANCE-

1   Trial balance

(a)   Identify the purpose of a trial balance.[k] **Ch 15**

(b)   Extract ledger balances into a trial balance.[s] **Ch 15**

(c)   Prepare extracts of an opening trial balance.[s] **Ch 15**

(d)   Identify and understand the limitations of a trial balance. [k] **Ch 15**

2   Correction of errors

(a)   Identify the types of error which may occur in bookkeeping systems.[k] **Ch 14,15**

(b)   Identify errors which would be highlighted by the extraction of a trial balance.[k] **Ch 15**

(c)   Prepare journal entries to correct errors.[s] **Ch 15**

(d)   Calculate and understand the impact of errors on the statement of profit or loss and other comprehensive income and statement of financial position.[s] **Ch 15**

3   Control accounts and reconciliations

(a)   Understand the purpose of control accounts for accounts receivable and accounts payable.[k] **Ch 14**

(b)   Understand how control accounts relate to the double entry system.[k] **Ch 14**

(c)   Prepare ledger control accounts from given information.[s] **Ch 14**

(d)   Perform control account reconciliations for accounts receivable and accounts payable.[s] **Ch 14**

(e)   Identify errors which would be highlighted by performing a control account reconciliation.[k] **Ch 14**

(f)   Identify and correct errors in control accounts and ledger accounts.[s] **Ch 14**

4   Bank reconciliations

(a)   Understand the purpose of bank reconciliations.[k] **Ch 14**

(b)   Identify the main reasons for differences between the cash book and the bank statement. [k] **Ch 14**

(c)   Correct cash book errors and/or omissions.[s] **Ch 14**

(d)   Prepare bank reconciliation statements. [s] **Ch 14**

(e)   Derive bank statement and cash book balances from given information.[s] **Ch 14**

(f)   Identify the bank balance to be reported in the final accounts.[s] **Ch 14**

5   Suspense accounts

(a)   Understand the purpose of a suspense account.[k] **Ch 15**

(b)   Identify errors leading to the creation of a suspense account. [k] **Ch 15**

(c)   Record entries in a suspense account. [s] **Ch 15**

(d)   Make journal entries to clear a suspense account. [s] **Ch 15**

F PREPARING BASIC FINANCIAL STATEMENTS

1   Statements of financial position

(a)   Recognise how the accounting equation, accounting treatments (as stipulated within sections D, E and examinable documents) and business entity convention underlie the statement of financial position.[k] **Ch 3 & 16**

(b)   Understand the nature of reserves.[k] **Ch 16**

(c)   Identify and report reserves in a company statement of financial position.[s]

(d)   Prepare statement of financial position or extracts as applicable from given information using accounting treatments as stipulated within sections D, E and examinable documents.[s] **Ch 16**

(e)   Understand why the heading retained earnings appears in a company statement of financial position.[k]   **Ch 16**

2   Statement of profit or loss and other comprehensive income

(a)   Prepare a statement of profit or loss and other comprehensive income or extracts as applicable from given information using accounting treatments as stipulated within sections D, E and examinable documents.[s] **Ch 16**

(b)   Understand how accounting concepts apply to revenue and expenses.[k] **Ch 1 & 16**

(c)   Calculate revenue, cost of sales, gross profit, profit for the year and total comprehensive income from given information.[s] **Ch 17**

(d)   Disclose items of income and expenditure in the statement of profit or loss.[s] **Ch 16**

(e)   Record income tax in the statement of profit or loss of a company, including the under and overprovision of tax in the prior year. [s] **Ch 13**

(f)   Understand the interrelationship between the statement of financial position and the statement of profit or loss and other comprehensive income. [k] **Ch 16**

(g)   Identify items requiring separate disclosure on the face of the statement of profit or loss.[k] **Ch 16**

3   Disclosure notes

(a)   Explain the purpose of disclosure notes.[k] **Ch 16**

(b)   Draft the following disclosure notes.[s]

   (i)   Non-current assets including tangible and   intangible assets **Ch 8**

   (ii)   Provisions **Ch 12**

   (iii)   Events after the reporting period **Ch 16**

   (iv)   Inventory **Ch 6**

4   Events after the reporting period

(a)   Define an event after the reporting period in accordance with International Financial Reporting Standards.[k] **Ch 16**

(b)   Classify events as adjusting or non-adjusting. [s]   **Ch 16**

(c)   Distinguish between how adjusting and non-adjusting events are reported in the financial statements. [k] **Ch 16**

5 **Statement of cash flow (excluding partnerships)**

(a) Differentiate between profit and cash flow.[k] **Ch 18**

(b) Understand the need for management to control cash flow. [k] **Ch 18**

(c) Recognise the benefits and drawbacks to users of the financial statements of a statement of cash flows.[k] **Ch 18**

(d) Classify the effect of transactions on cash flows.[s] **Ch 18**

(e) Calculate the figures needed for the statement of cash flows including:[s] **Ch 18**

    (i) cash flows from operating activities

    (ii) cash flows from investing activities

    (iii) cash flows from financing activities.

(f) Calculate the cash flow from operating activities using the indirect and direct method.[s] **Ch 18**

(g) Prepare statement of cash flows and extracts from statements of cash flows from given information.[s] **Ch 18**

(h) Identify the treatment of given transactions in a company's statement of cash flows. [k] **Ch 18**

6 **Incomplete records**

(a) Understand and apply techniques used in incomplete record situations:[s] **Ch 17**

    (i) use of accounting equation

    (ii) use of ledger accounts to calculate missing figures

    (iii) use of cash and/or bank summaries

    (iv) use of profit percentages to calculate missing figures.

G PREPARING SIMPLE CONSOLIDATED FINANCIAL STATEMENTS

1 **Subsidiaries**

(a) Define and describe the following terms in the context of group accounting.[k] **Ch 20**

    (i) Parent

    (ii) Subsidiary

    (iii) Control

    (iv) Consolidated or group financial statements

    (v) Non-controlling interest

    (vi) Trade/simple investment

(b) Identify subsidiaries within a group structure. [k] **Ch 20**

(c) Describe the components of and prepare a consolidated statement of financial position or extracts thereof including.[s] **Ch 20**

    (i) Fair value adjustments at acquisition on land and buildings (excluding depreciation adjustments)

    (ii) Fair value of consideration transferred from cash and shares (excluding deferred and contingent consideration)

    (iii) Elimination of intra-group trading balances (excluding cash and goods in transit)

    (iv) Removal of unrealised profit arising on intra-group trading

    (v) acquisition of subsidiaries part way through the financial year

(d) Calculate goodwill (excluding impairment of goodwill) using the full goodwill method only as follows:[s] **Ch 20**

Fair value of consideration	X
Fair value of non-controlling interest	X
Less fair value of net assets at acquisition	(X)
Goodwill at acquisition	X

(e) Describe the components of and prepare a consolidated statement of profit or loss or extracts thereof including:[s] **Ch 21**

    (i) Elimination of intra-group trading balances (excluding cash and goods in transit)

    (ii) Removal of unrealised profit arising on intra-group trading

    (iii) Acquisition of subsidiaries part way through the financial year

2 Associates

(a) Define and identify an associate and significant influence and identify the situations where significant influence or participating interest exists.[k] **Ch 21**

(b) Describe the key features of a parent-associate relationship and be able to identify an associate within a group structure. [k] **Ch 21**

(c) Describe the principle of equity accounting. [k] **Ch 21**

H INTERPRETATION OF FINANCIAL STATEMENTS

1 Importance and purpose of analysis of financial statements

(a) Describe how the interpretation and analysis of financial statements is used in a business environment. [k] **Ch 19**

(b) Explain the purpose of interpretation of ratios.[k] **Ch 19**

2 Ratios

(a) Calculate key accounting ratios.[s] **Ch 19**

    (i) Profitability

    (ii) Liquidity

    (iii) Efficiency

    (iv) Position

(b) Explain the interrelationships between ratios. [k] **Ch 19**

3 Analysis of financial statements

(a) Calculate and interpret the relationship between the elements of the financial statements with regard to profitability, liquidity, efficient use of resources and financial position.[s] **Ch 19**

(b) Draw valid conclusions from the information contained within the financial statements and present these to the appropriate user of the financial statements.[s] **Ch 19**

TOP 10 TIPS TO IMPROVE YOUR RESULT

Be organised and plan your study time – there are more tips on how to do this below.

'Mens sana in corpore sano' – prepare your body; sleep well and eat right as a healthy body leads to a healthy mind!

Study according to your learning style – different people have different learning styles. Some people are visual learners, some people prefer sound, some need physical motion – try out different methods to see what works best for you.

Try using a study buddy – this could be someone taking the same exam, or a friend or family member.

Revise knowledge efficiently – stay focused, stop procrastinating and don't let your mind wander.

Read questions very carefully – many students fail to answer the actual question set. Read the question once right through and then again more slowly. Make note of key words in the question when you read through it.

Ensure you know the structure of the exam – how many questions (and of what type) you will be expected to answer. During your revision, attempt all the different styles of questions you may be asked.

Be a good test-taker. Get lots of practice – the ACCA release sample assessments and practice CBE mock exams are available.

Read good newspapers and professional journals, especially ACCA's *Student Accountant* – this can give you a distinct advantage in the exam.

Adopt a positive mental attitude. You may have nerves and feel anxious but with the correct preparation and practice you can have confidence in your ability to succeed.

PLAN YOUR STUDY TIME

Decide which times of the week you will devote to revising.

Put the times you plan to revise onto a study plan for the weeks from now until the exam and set yourself targets for each period of revision, ensuring that you cover the whole syllabus.

If you are studying for more than one paper at a time, try to mix and match your subjects as this can help you to keep motivated and see each subject in its broader context.

When working through your course, compare your progress with your plan and, if you fall behind, re-plan your work (perhaps including extra sessions). If you are ahead, do some extra revision/practice questions.

EXTRA QUESTIONS

Practising exam standard questions is a critical part of your revision.

Specimen Exams and Practice Tests are available from http://www.accaglobal.com/gb/en/student/exam-support-resources.html

and Exam Kits and Mock Exams in the style of the real exam can be obtained from

http://kaplan-publishing.kaplan.co.uk/acca-books/pages/acca-books.aspx.

1 Introduction to financial reporting

The following topics are covered in this chapter:

- Overview of accounting
- The users of financial statements
- Types of business entities
- The framework
- Qualitative characteristics
- Elements of the financial statements
- Other important accounting concepts

1.1 OVERVIEW OF ACCOUNTING

LEARNING SUMMARY

After studying this section you should be able to:

- outline the purpose of the accounting system and the financial statements
- identify the differences between financial and management accounting.

The accounting system of a business records and summarises the financial position and performance of the business. The summarised information is then presented in the form of financial statements.

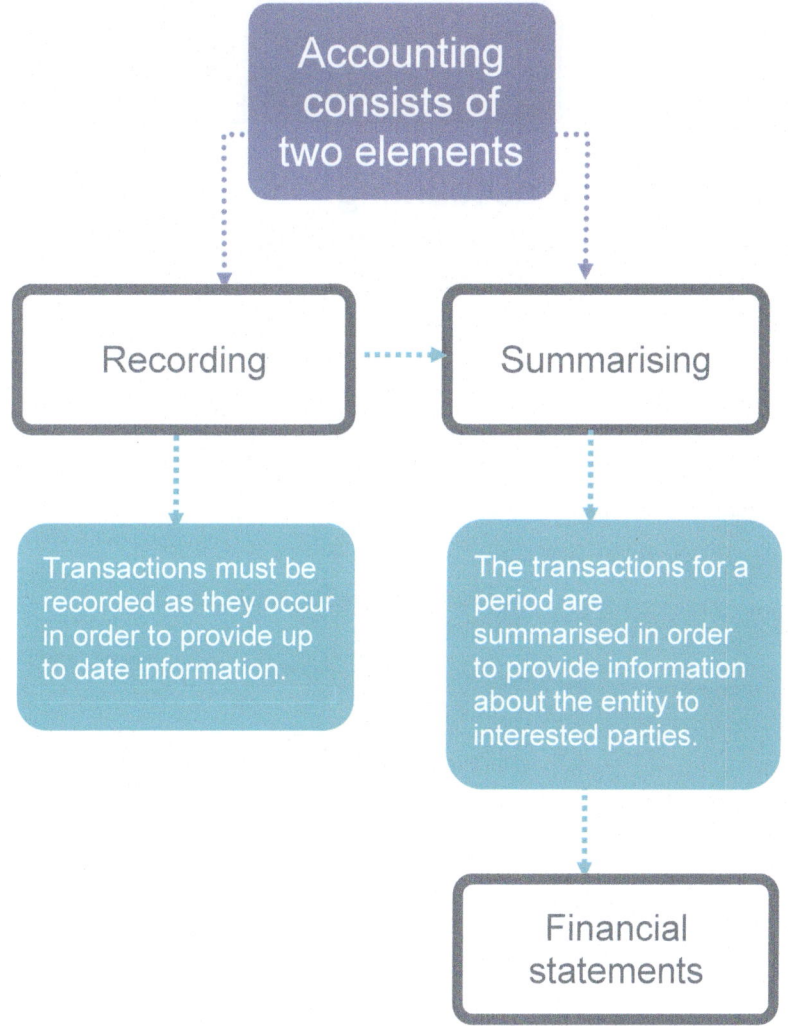

Accounting consists of two elements

Recording

Summarising

Transactions must be recorded as they occur in order to provide up to date information.

The transactions for a period are summarised in order to provide information about the entity to interested parties.

Financial statements

The financial statements

Financial statements are made up of:

The statement of financial position

This statement summarises the assets, liabilities and equity balances of the business at the end of the reporting period.

The statement of changes in equity

This statement summarises the movement in equity balances i.e. share capital, share premium, revaluation surplus and retained earnings during the reporting period..

The statement of profit or loss

This statement summarises the revenues earned and expenses incurred by the business throughout the reporting period.

The statement of cash flows

This statement summarises the cash paid and received throughout the reporting period.

The notes to the financial statements

The notes to the financial statements comprise a statement of accounting policies and any other disclosures required to enable to the shareholders and other users of the financial statements to make informed judgements about the business.

> The preparation of these statements is reviewed later in the text.

Financial vs management accounting

Financial accounting	Management accounting
Production of summary financial statements for external users.	Production of detailed accounts, used by management to control the business and plan for the future.
Usually prepared annually.	Normally prepared monthly, often on a rolling basis.
Generally required by law.	Not mandatory.
Reflects past performance and position.	Includes budgets and forecasts of future activities, as well as reflecting past performance.
Information calculated and presented in accordance with international accounting standards.	Information prepared and presented in order to be relevant to managers.

> It is crucial to have an understanding of the two functions of financial and management accounting and their differences.

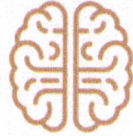

Do you understand?

1   Accounting can be described as the recording and summarising of transactions.

True or false?

2   Which one of the following sentences does NOT explain the distinction between financial statements and management accounts?

    A   Financial statements are primarily for external users and management accounts are primarily for internal users.

    B   Financial statements are normally produced annually and management accounts are normally produced monthly.

    C   Financial statements are more accurate than management accounts.

    D   Financial statements are audited by an external auditor and management accounts do not normally have an external audit.

1   True
2   C Both financial and management accounts should be equally accurate and reliable

1.2   USERS OF THE FINANCIAL STATEMENTS

LEARNING SUMMARY

After studying this section you should be able to:

- identify the users of financial statements and differentiate between their information needs.

User	Interest?
Investors	What are the potential profits and the security of their investment?
Customers	Can they continue to be supplied in the future?
Suppliers	Will they be paid? Can they be reassured about the financial health of a business before agreeing to supply goods?
Lenders	Will they be repaid?
Government	How is the economy performing? What is the amount of tax payable by a business?
Competitors	What strategy should be taken? How does their performance and position compare?
The public	What is the impact on the economy, local environment and local community?
Employees	Is employment secure? Is a pay rise or bonus possible?
Management	What are the operational and strategic decisions?

Each user will have their own reasons for their interest in the financial statements.

3

Do you understand?

1   Which one of the following user groups is likely to require the most detailed financial information?

    A   The management

    B   Investors and potential investors

    C   Government agencies

    D   Employees

1   A Management require very detailed information in order to make informed decisions with regard to operations

1.3   TYPES OF BUSINESS ENTITIES

LEARNING SUMMARY

After studying this section you should be able to:

- Identify and define types of business entity.

A **sole trader** is a business entity which is owned and operated by one individual.	• In law there is no distinction between the owner and the business. • The sole trader has personal unlimited liability for the business debts and losses.
A **partnership** is a business entity which is owned and operated by more than one individual.	• The partners will share the profits. • The partners have personal unlimited liability for the business debts and losses.
A **company** is an incorporated business owned by shareholders who have invested capital in return for a shareholding.	• A legal entity distinct from its owners. • Limited liability – shareholders are not personally liable for the business debts. • Return on their investment in the company referred to as a dividend.

1.4 THE FRAMEWORK

Regulatory bodies are reviewed in chapter 2.

One of the most important documents underpinning the preparation of financial statements is the Conceptual Framework for Financial Reporting ('the Framework'), which was prepared by the International Accounting Standards Board.

The Framework presents the main ideas, concepts and principles upon which International Financial Reporting Standards are based.

KEY POINT The main objective of financial reporting is to present information that users can base their decision making on.

Fair presentation

Fair presentation concerns the financial information being 'true and fair'.

A **true and fair** view

A 'true and fair' view has not been formally defined but embodies:

* compliance with relevant laws and regulations
* compliance with the relevant financial reporting framework
* the application of the qualitative characteristics of the Framework.

1.5 QUALITATIVE CHARACTERISTICS

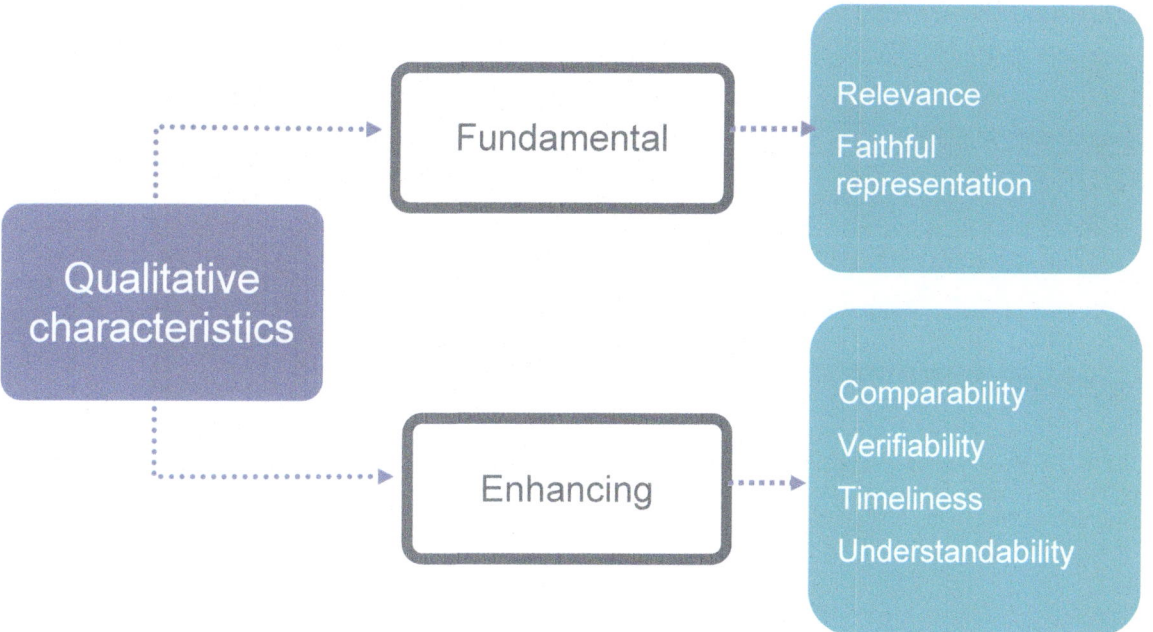

Fundamental qualitative characteristics	
Relevance	It influences the economic decisions of users by helping them evaluate past, present or future events or confirming or correcting their past evaluations.
Faithful representation	Transactions and other events must be accounted for and presented in accordance with their substance and economic reality and not merely their legal form.

Enhancing qualitative characteristics	
Comparability	Users must be able to compare financial statements over a period of time to identify trends and to compare financial statements of different entities to be able to assess their relative financial position and performance.
Verifiability	Can be direct or indirect. Direct verification means verifying through direct observation. Indirect verification means checking the inputs to a model, formula or other technique and recalculating the outputs using the same methodology.
Timeliness	Information made available to decision makers in time to be capable of influencing their decisions
Understandability	Readily understandable by users, although relevant information should never be excluded due to being considered too difficult for some users.

1.6 ELEMENTS OF THE FINANCIAL STATEMENTS

LEARNING SUMMARY

After studying this section you should be able to:

- identify and define the elements that make up the financial statements

- classify items as current or non-current assets or liabilities.

KEY POINT The financial statements must summarise five key elements in order to reflect the financial position and performance

Statement of profit or loss	Statement of financial position	
Income	Assets	
Expense	Liability	
	Equity	

It is important to know which elements appear in each of the financial statements.

DEFINITION An **asset** is 'a resource owned or controlled by an entity as a result of past events and from which future economic benefits are expected to flow to the entity' (Framework, Glossary)

DEFINITION A **liability** is 'a present obligation arising from past events, the settlement of which is expected to result in an outflow from the entity of resources embodying economic benefits' (Framework, Glossary)

DEFINITION **Capital/equity** is a special kind of liability due to the owner(s) and is 'the residual interest in the assets of the entity after deducting all its liabilities' (Framework, para 4.4)

DEFINITION **Income** 'increases in economic benefits during the accounting period in the form of inflows or enhancements of assets or decreases of liabilities that result in an increase in equity' (Framework, Glossary)

DEFINITION **Expense** 'decreases in economic benefits during the accounting period in the form of outflows or diminutions of assets or increases of liabilities that result in a decrease in equity' (Framework, Para 4.25)

Categorisation of assets and liabilities

Assets and liabilities need to be classified according to the length of time they are employed in the business.

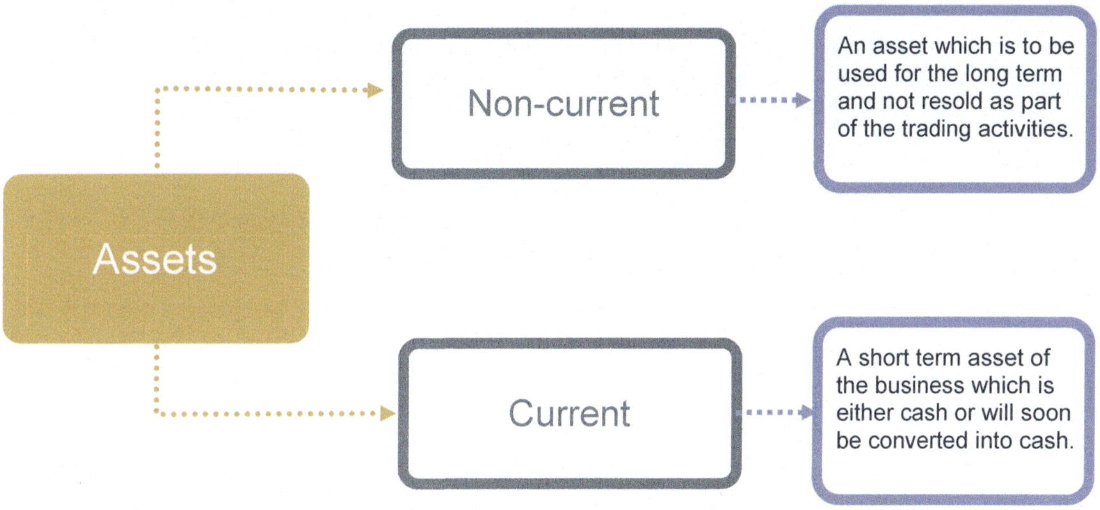

Assets

Non-current → An asset which is to be used for the long term and not resold as part of the trading activities.

Current → A short term asset of the business which is either cash or will soon be converted into cash.

DEFINITION A tangible asset has physical substance. A non-tangible asset has no physical substance.

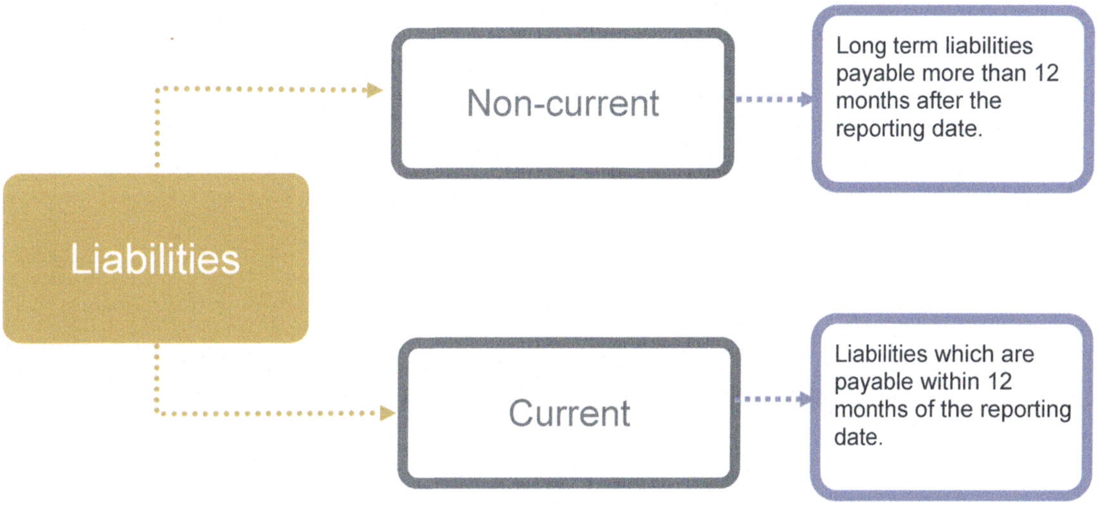

Liabilities

Non-current → Long term liabilities payable more than 12 months after the reporting date.

Current → Liabilities which are payable within 12 months of the reporting date.

1.7 OTHER IMPORTANT ACCOUNTING CONCEPTS

LEARNING SUMMARY

After studying this section you should be able to:

- define, understand and apply accounting concepts.

Materiality	An item is regarded as material if its omission or misstatement is likely to change the perception or understanding of the user of that information.
Substance over form	If information is to be presented faithfully, the economic reality must be accounted for and not just the strict legal form.
Going concern	Financial statements are prepared on the basis that the entity will continue to trade for the foreseeable future.
The business entity	Financial accounting information presented in the financial statements relates only to activities of the business and not to those of the owner.
The accruals basis	Transactions are recorded when revenues are earned and when expenses are incurred. This pays no regard to the timing of cash payment or receipt.
Fair presentation	Relates to preparation of the financial statements in accordance with applicable financial reporting standards, together with relevant laws and regulation.
Consistence	Users of the financial statements need to be able to compare the performance of a company over a number of years and so classification and presentation of items should be retained from one period to the next.

Do you understand?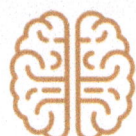

1. Classify the following into whether they are non-current and current assets and liabilities.

    (i) Land & buildings (ii) receivables (iii) cash in hand (iv) loan repayable in three years' time

2. The concept of materiality means that businesses will only report material transactions, balances and events. True or false?

3. Faithful representation means that the commercial effect of a transaction must always be shown in the financial statements even if this differs from legal form. True or false?

1. (i) Land & buildings – non-current asset (ii) receivables – current asset (iii) cash in hand – current asset (iv) loan repayable in three years' time – non-current liability
2. False - Businesses should report all transactions, events and balances in their financial statements. Materiality is simply a measure for determining how significant that information is to users.
3. True – Faithful representation includes the concept that transactions should reflect their economic substance, rather than the legal form of the transaction.

1   **What is the main purpose of financial accounting?**

    A   To record all transactions in the books of account

    B   To provide management with detailed analyses of costs

    C   To enable preparation of financial statements that provides information about an entity's financial performance and position

    D   To calculate profit or loss for an accounting period

2   **Which one of the following statements best defines a liability?**

    A   A liability is an obligation arising from a past transaction or event.

    B   A liability is a legally binding amount owed to a third party.

    C   A liability is an obligation arising from a past transaction or event which is expected to be settled by an outflow of economic benefits.

    D   A liability is anything which results in an outflow of economic benefits from an entity.

3   **Which one of the following statements best defines an asset?**

    A   An asset is a resource owned by the entity with a financial value.

    B   An asset is a resource controlled by an entity from which future economic benefits are expected to be generated.

    C   An asset is a resource controlled by an entity as a result of past events.

    D   An asset is a resource controlled by an entity as a result of past events from which future economic benefits are expected to be generated.

4   **Which of the following items is not an enhancing qualitative characteristic of useful financial information as stated in the IASB Framework?**

    A   Comparability

    B   Timeliness

    C   Faithful representation

    D   Understandability

5   **Which two of the following items are enhancing qualitative characteristics of useful financial information as stated in the IASB Framework?**

A   Relevance

B   Comparability

C   Faithful representation

D   Verifiability

2 The regulatory framework

The following topics are covered in this chapter:

- The regulatory framework
- Company ownership and control
- Corporate governance

2.1 THE REGULATORY FRAMEWORK

LEARNING SUMMARY

After studying this section you should be able to:

- understand the role of the regulatory system
- understand the role of International Financial Reporting Standards (IFRS Standards®).

Why is a regulatory framework necessary?

A regulatory framework is required for the preparation of financial statements in order:

To meet the information needs of users
To ensure information is comparable and consistent
To increase users' confidence in the financial reporting process
To regulate the behaviour of companies and directors

Structure of the international regulatory system

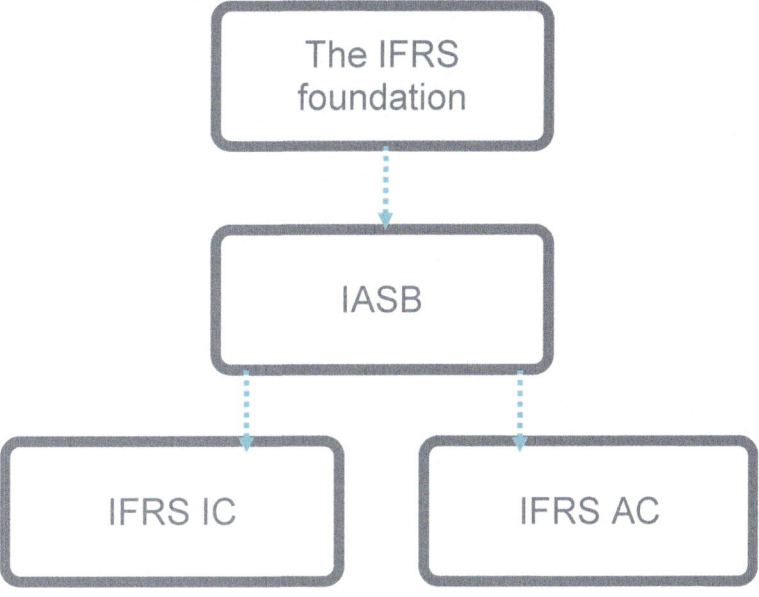

The IFRS foundation
The Foundation is the supervisory body for the IASB® and is responsible for governance issues and ensuring each member body is properly funded.

Bring about the convergence of national and international financial reporting standards.

Develop a set of high quality, understandable, enforceable and globally accepted financial reporting standards.

IFRS foundation's objectives

Take account of the financial reporting needs of emerging economies and small and medium sized entities.

Promote the use and rigorous application of those standards.

International Accounting Standards Board (IASB®)
The Board is the independent standard setting body of the Foundation.

Its members are responsible for the development and publication of IFRS Standards and interpretations developed by the Interpretations Committee (IFRIC® Interpretations). Upon its creation the Board also adopted all existing International Accounting Standards (IAS® Standards).

All of the most important national standard setters are represented on the Board and their views are taken into account so that a consensus can be reached. All national standard setters can issue discussion papers and exposure drafts issued by the Board for comment in their own countries, so that the views of all preparers and users of financial statements can be represented. Each major national standard setter 'leads' certain international standard-setting projects.

The IFRS Interpretations Committee
The IFRIC reviews widespread accounting issues (in the context of IFRS Standards) on a timely basis and provides authoritative guidance on these issues.

The IFRS Advisory Council
The Council is the formal advisory body to the Board and the Foundation.

Advising the Board on agenda decisions and priorities in their work.

IFRS Advisory Council's objectives

Giving other advice to the Board or to the Trustees.

Informing the Board of the views of the Council with regard to major standard-setting projects.

2.2 COMPANY OWNERSHIP AND CONTROL

LEARNING SUMMARY

After studying this section you should be able to:

- understand the delegation of control within a company.

Directors are appointed to manage the business on behalf of the owners. This leads to the separation of ownership and control within the company.

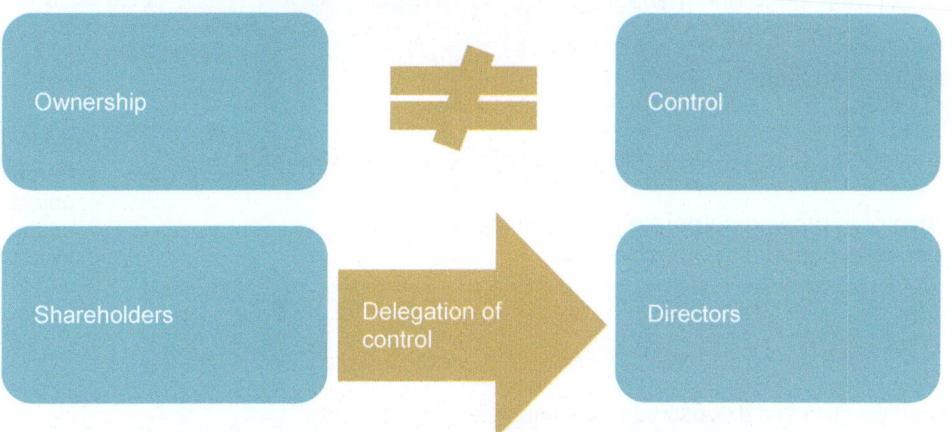

2.3 CORPORATE GOVERNANCE

LEARNING SUMMARY

After studying this section you should be able to: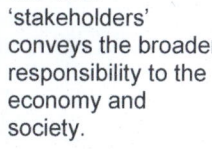

- describe the purposes and objectives of corporate governance
- understand the need for corporate governance.

The term 'stakeholders' conveys the broader responsibility to the economy and society.

DEFINITION The Cadbury Report 1992 defines corporate governance as 'the system by which companies are directed and controlled' in the interests of shareholders and stakeholders.

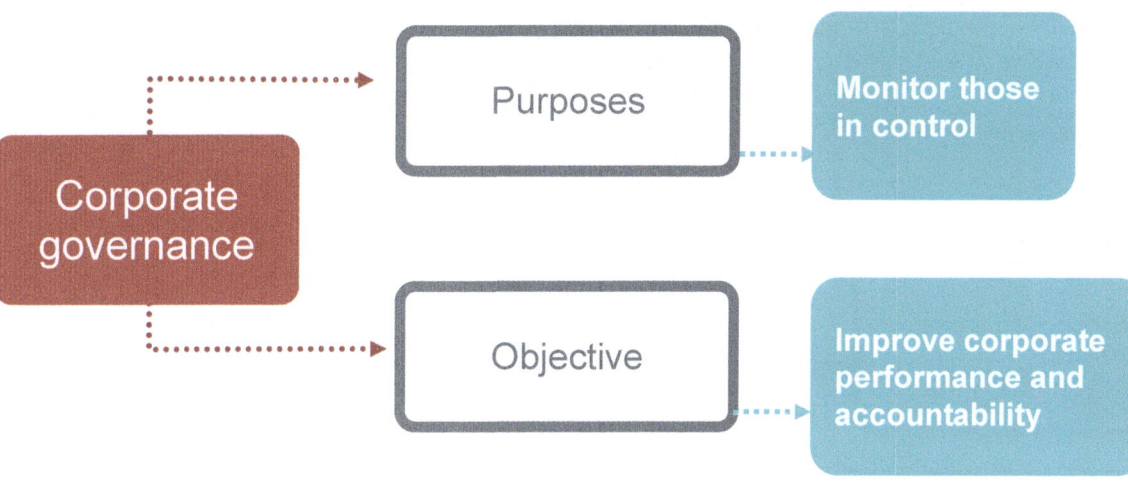

The primary purpose of monitoring those in control has several supporting purposes:

Supporting purposes:
Ensure there is a suitable balance of power on the board of directors.
Fair remuneration for executive directors.
Assign responsibility of monitoring and managing risk to the directors.
Ensure auditors are independent.
Address other issues such as; corporate social responsibility and business ethics.

The primary objective of improving corporate performance and accountability has several supporting objectives:

Supporting objectives:
Increase the amount of reporting and disclosures to stakeholders.
Increase levels of confidence and transparency.
Ensure business is run legally and ethically.
Ensure auditors are independent.
Promote control that cascades through the organisation.

Purposes and objectives are based on the needs to 'direct' and 'control'

The need for corporate governance

There needs to be a system that ensures publically owned companies are run in the interests of the shareholders and that provides adequate accountability of the people managing those companies.

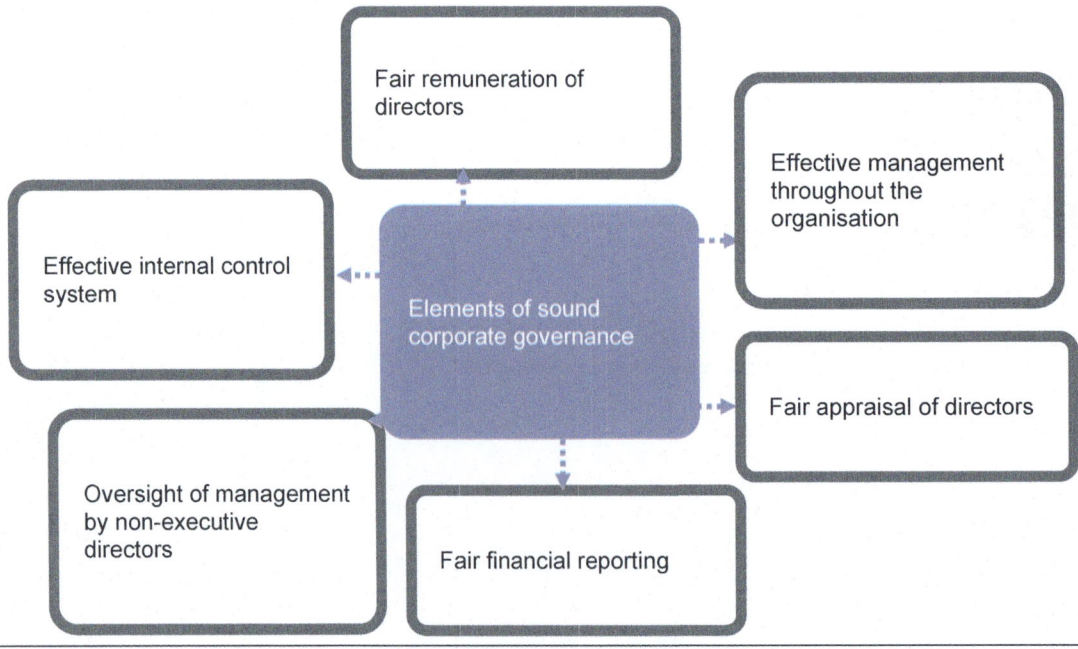

Do you understand?

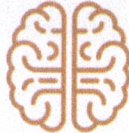

1   The IFRS Advisory Council is the formal advisory body to the Board and the Foundation.

     True or false?

2   The regulatory framework has the objective of regulating the behaviour of the shareholders.

     True or false?

3   Which one of the following items could be used to best encourage executive directors to operate in the best interests of the company?

     (i)   A high salary

     (ii)   Bonuses based on company and individual performance

3   (ii)
2   False
1   True

1   Which body is responsible for the issue of International Financial Reporting Standards?

A   The IFRS Advisory Council

B   The International Financial Reporting Interpretations Committee

C   The International Accounting Standards Board

D   The European Union

2   Which of the following statements relating to the IASB's Conceptual Framework for Financial Reporting 'the Framework' are true?

(1)   The Framework is an accounting standard.

(2)   The Framework assists in harmonising global accounting practices.

(3)   The Framework assists national standard setters to develop national standards.

(4)   The Framework assists users of financial information to interpret financial statements.

A   (1) and (2)

B   (2), (3) and (4)

C   All four

D   (1) and (3)

3   Which one of the following items is the most obvious means of achieving public oversight of corporate governance?

A   The company establishing a comprehensive web site

B   Publication of the Annual Report and Accounts

C   Press announcements of all significant developments

D   Shareholder access to the Annual General Meeting

3 Double entry bookkeeping

The following topics are covered in this chapter:

- Business transactions and the accounting system
- Business documentation
- Day books & the journal
- Duality and the accounting equation

3.1 BUSINESS TRANSACTIONS AND THE ACCOUNTING SYSTEM

LEARNING SUMMARY

After studying this section you should be able to:

- outline the accounting system for the recording of business transactions.

The purpose of accounting is to record and classify business transactions. A business may enter into a large number of transactions on a daily basis. It is quite clear that keeping track of all these transactions can be a detailed process.

To ensure that a business does keep track of all sales earned, purchases and expenses incurred, the transactions are recorded in an accounting system.

Overview of the accounting system

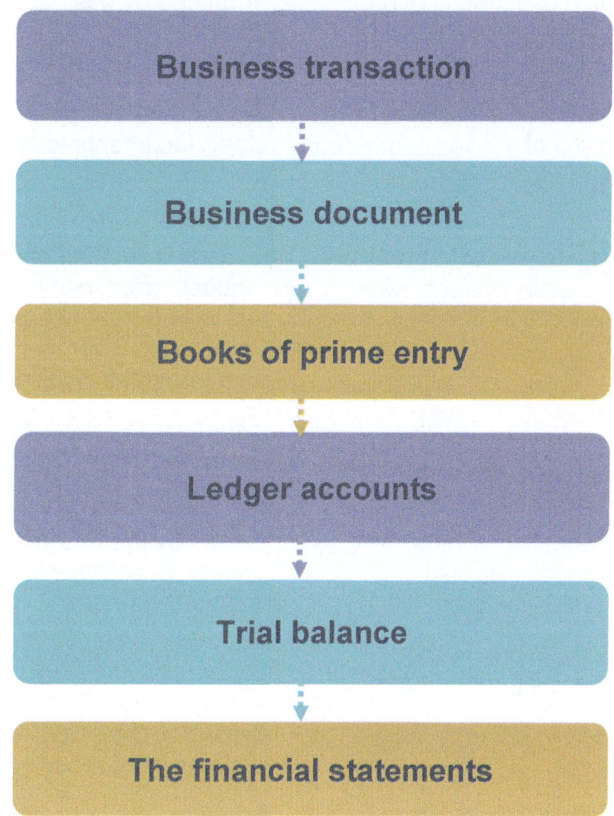

3.2 BUSINESS DOCUMENTATION

LEARNING SUMMARY

After studying this section you should be able to:

- outline the purpose and content of a number of business documents.

Various documents may be used when dealing with different business transactions. The table below summarises the main types of business documentation and sources of data for an accounting system together with their content and purpose.

Documentation	Contents	Purpose
Quotation	Quantity/description/details of goods required.	To establish price from various suppliers.
Purchase order	Details of supplier, e.g. name, address, quantity ordered, price, terms and conditions etc.	Sent to supplier as a request for supply.
Sales order	Quantity/description/details of goods required and price.	Cross checked with order placed with customer. Sent to stores/warehouse to process the order.
Dispatch note (GDN)	Details of supplier, e.g. name and address. Quantity and description of goods.	Provided by supplier. Checked with goods received and purchase order.
Goods received note (GRN)	Quantity and description of goods.	Produced by business receiving the goods as proof of receipt. Matched with delivery note.
Statement	Details of supplier e.g. name and address, date and invoice numbers, payments made, amounts owing etc.	Issued by the supplier. Checked with other documents to ensure amount owing is correct.
Invoice	Name and address of supplier and customer, details of goods, e.g. quantity, price, value sales tax etc.	Issued by supplier of goods as a request for payment. For the supplier this will be treated as a sales invoice. For the customer this will be treated as a purchase invoice.
Credit note	Details of supplier, details of goods returned e.g. quantity, price, value etc.	Issued by the supplier. Checked with documents regarding goods returned.
Debit note	Details of supplier. Contains details of goods returned e.g. quantity, price, value etc.	Issued by the business receiving the goods. Cross checked to credit note issued by supplier.
Remittance advice	Method of payment, invoice number, account number etc.	Sent to supplier as notification of payment.
Receipt	Details of payment received.	Issued by the seller indicating that payment was received.

3.3 DAY BOOKS AND THE JOURNAL

LEARNING SUMMARY

After studying this section you should be able to:

- identify the books of prime entry and their purpose.

Transactions are initially recorded in a book of prime entry. This is a simple record of the transaction, the relevant customer/supplier and the amount of the transaction. It is, in essence, a list of daily transactions in date order. Several books of prime entry exist, each record a different type of transaction:

> Books of prime entry can also be referred to as 'day books'.

Book of prime entry	Transaction type
Sales day book	Credit sales
Purchases day book	Credit purchases
Sales returns day book	Return of goods sold on credit
Purchases returns day book	Return of goods bought on credit
Cash book	All bank transactions
Petty cash book	All small cash transactions
The journal	All transactions not recorded in any other day book such as; • the purchase and sale of non-current assets • recording the annual depreciation charge • the write-off of irrecoverable debts • allowances for receivables • accruals and prepayments • transfers between accounts • the correction of errors.

3.4 DUALITY AND THE ACCOUNTING EQUATION

LEARNING SUMMARY

After studying this section you should be able to:

- understand and apply the concept of double entry accounting and the duality concept

- understand and apply the accounting equation

- identify and understand the steps to record accounting transactions.

Duality

To follow the rules of double entry bookkeeping, each time a transaction is recorded, both effects must be taken into account. These two effects are equal and opposite and, as such, the accounting equation will always balance.

The accounting equation

Assets = Equity + Liabilities

The accounting equation is a simple expression that at any point in time the assets of the business will be equal to its liabilities plus the equity of the business.

Steps to record a transaction

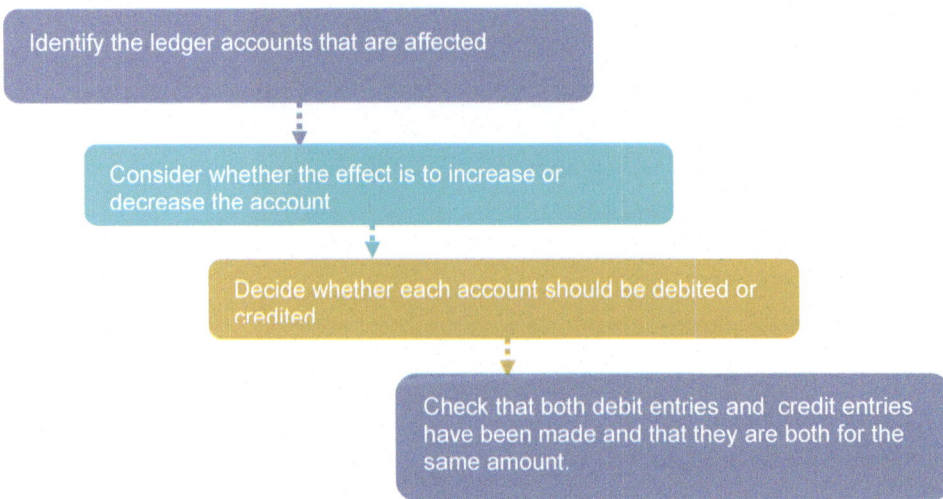

Identify the ledger accounts that are affected

Consider whether the effect is to increase or decrease the account

Decide whether each account should be debited or credited

Check that both debit entries and credit entries have been made and that they are both for the same amount.

Decide whether a debit or credit entry is required by using the 'PEARLS' mnemonic set out below.

Whether an entry is to the debit or credit side of an account depends on the type of account and the transaction:

Ledger account	
A **debit entry** represents:	A **credit entry** represents:
An increase to an asset	An increase to a liability
A decrease to a liability	A decrease to an asset
An increase to an item of expense	An increase to an item of income
A decrease to an item of income	A decrease to an item of expense

Debit can be shortened to 'Dr' and credit can be shortened to 'Cr'.

For increases to the ledger accounts, we can remember this as the mnemonic **'PEARLS':**

Debit	Credit
Increase in:	Increase in:
Purchases	**R**evenues
Expenses	**L**iabilities
Assets	**S**hareholders' equity

Do you understand?

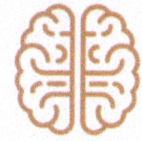

1   A debit entry increases an asset.

    True or false?

2   A credit entry increases an expense.

    True or false?

3   State the accounting equation.

4   Describe the content and purpose of an invoice.

5   Describe the content and purpose of a purchase order.

1   True
2   False
3   Assets = Equity + Liabilities
4   Purpose of an invoice – a request for payment issued by the supplier of goods or service. Content of an invoice - name and address of supplier and customer, details of goods or service, e.g. quantity, price, value sales tax etc.
5   Purpose of a purchase order – a request for supply sent to a supplier. Content of a purchase order - details of supplier, e.g. name, address, quantity ordered, price, terms and conditions etc.

1   **Which one of the following statements best describes the purpose of a goods despatched note (delivery note)?**

   A   It is issued by a customer returning faulty goods to their supplier.

   B   It is issued by a customer to their supplier and specifies the quantity and type of goods they require to be despatched.

   C   It is issued by a supplier to their customer and specifies the quantity and type of goods delivered to that customer.

   D   It is issued by a supplier to their customer and specifies what goods will be provided to them at a specified future date.

2   **An invoice is best defined by which one of the following statements?**

   A   An invoice is raised by a business and confirms only the amount due to be paid for goods and services provided.

   B   An invoice is raised by business and issued to a supplier as recognition of goods and services received from that supplier.

   C   An invoice is raised by a business and issued to a customer to confirm amounts not yet paid.

   D   An invoice is raised by a business and issued to a customer to request payment for goods and services provided.

3   **With regard to the journal, state which of the following statements is true.**

   A   The journal records all bank and cash transactions

   B   The journal records all accounting transactions

   C   The journal is a book of prime entry

   D   The journal records all credit sales transactions

4   **Which of the following are books of prime entry?**

   A   Sales day book and trial balance

   B   Petty cash book and accounts receivables ledger

   C   Petty cash book and journal

   D   Purchase day book and accounts payable ledger

5   **Which one of the following statements best describes the purpose of a purchase order?**

   A   It is issued to a supplier to request supply of goods from them on terms specified within the order.

   B   It is issued to a customer to confirm the supply of goods to them on terms specified in the order.

   C   It is issued to a supplier as notification of payment.

   D   It confirms the price that will be charged by a supplier for goods supplied.

4 **Ledger accounting**

The following topics are covered in this chapter:

- Ledger accounts
- Recording cash and credit transactions
- Balancing off the ledger accounts
- Closing off the ledger accounts

4.1 LEDGER ACCOUNTS

LEARNING SUMMARY

After studying this section you should be able to:

- understand what the general ledger is
- describe the format of a ledger account.

> **DEFINITION** A **ledger account** is an account that records transactions relating to a particular item.

The general ledger

The general ledger contains all of the accounts necessary to summarise an entity's transactions and prepare the financial statements - the statement of financial position and the statement of profit or loss.

There is no rule as to how many ledger accounts an entity should have but the system should facilitate effective and efficient accounting and control.

The format of a ledger account

Each ledger account comprises two sides: the left hand side is referred to as the debit side and the right hand side is referred to as the credit side.

> The date columns contain the date of the transaction.

> The title of the account is a name that reflects the nature of the transaction.

> A ledger account may also be referred to as a T-account.

Title of account					
Date	Details	Amount $	Date	Details	Amount $

> The amount columns contain the value of the transaction.

> The details columns contain the title of the other account(s) that hold the opposite side of the dual effect i.e. opposite account affected.

> **KEY POINT** We post entries to the debit or credit sides dependent on whether they are increases or decreases to an account.

4.2 RECORDING CASH AND CREDIT TRANSACTIONS

LEARNING SUMMARY

After studying this section you should be able to:

- define cash and credit transactions
- record sales and purchases on a cash and credit basis.

Recording cash transactions

DEFINITION Cash transactions are those where payment is made or received immediately.

When cash is received (i.e. receipt of an asset) the entry in the cash ledger is a debit. When cash is paid out (i.e. a reduction in an asset) the entry in the cash ledger is a credit.

Recording credit transactions

DEFINITION Credit transactions are those where goods or services are sold and purchased and paid for at a later date.

Money that a business is owed is accounted for in the receivables ledger (increase in an asset).

Money that a business owes is accounted for in the payables ledger (increase in a liability).

Recording sales and purchases on a cash and credit basis

Cash sale	
Dr	Cash
Cr	Sales
Credit sale	
Dr	Receivables
Cr	Sales
Cash purchase	
Dr	Purchases
Cr	Cash
Credit purchase	
Dr	Purchases
Cr	Payables

4.3 BALANCING OFF THE LEDGER ACCOUNTS

LEARNING SUMMARY

After studying this section you should be able to:

- understand the process of balancing off ledger accounts.

Total both sides of the T-account and find the larger total.

Put the larger total in the total box on the debit and credit side.

Insert a balancing figure to the side of the T-account which does not currently add up to the amount in the total box. Call this balancing figure 'balance c/f' (carried forward) or 'balance c/d' (carried down).

Carry the balance down diagonally and call it 'balance b/f' (brought forward) or 'balance b/d' (brought down).

4.4 CLOSING OFF THE LEDGER ACCOUNTS

LEARNING SUMMARY

After studying this section you should be able to:

- understand the process of closing off ledger accounts.

At the end of the accounting period, the ledger accounts must be closed off in preparation for the recording of transactions in the next accounting period.

Statement of financial position

Assets and liabilities at the end of a period = Assets and liabilities at start of the next period.

Balance c/f = asset or liability at the end of the accounting period.

Balance b/f = asset or liability at the start of the next accounting period.

Statement of profit or loss

At the end of a period any amounts that relate to that period are transferred out of the income and expenditure accounts into another ledger account called profit or loss.

Do not show a balance c/f or balance b/f but instead put the balancing figure on the smallest side and label it 'profit or loss'.

Do you understand?

1   What is the accounting entry to record a cash purchase?

2   What is the accounting entry to record a cash sale?

3   The entry to record a credit sale is:

Dr Payables

Cr Sales

True or false?

4   Describe the process of balancing off a ledger account.

---

1   Dr Purchases Cr Cash
2   Dr Cash Cr Sales
3   False. The accounting entry for a credit sale is: Dr Receivables Cr Sales
4   The process of balancing off a ledger account:
Step 1: Total both sides of the T-account and find the larger total.
Step 2: Put the larger total in the total box on the debit and credit side.
Step 3: Insert a balancing figure to the side of the T-account which does not currently add up to the amount in the total box. Call this balancing figure 'balance c/f' (carried forward) or 'balance c/d' (carried down).
Step 4: Carry the balance down diagonally and call it 'balance b/f' (brought forward) or 'balance b/d' (brought down).

Exam style questions

1   The double-entry system of bookkeeping normally results in which of the following balances on the ledger accounts?

	Debit balances:	Credit balances:
A	Assets and revenues	Liabilities, capital and expenses
B	Revenues, capital and liabilities	Assets and expenses
C	Assets and expenses	Liabilities, capital and revenues
D	Assets, expenses and capital	Liabilities and revenues

2   Which one of the following statements is correct?

A   Assets and liabilities normally have credit balances

B   Liabilities and revenues normally have debit balances

C   Assets and revenues normally have credit balances

D   Assets and expenses normally have debit balances

3   Tick the appropriate column in the table below to show in which financial statement each of the elements listed would be included.

Element	Statement of profit or loss	Statement of financial position
Assets		
Liabilities		
Expenses		
Income		
Equity		

4 **Tick the correct boxes in the table below to show whether each of the following transactions would require a debit or a credit entry.**

	Debit	Credit
Increases in capital/equity		
Increase in assets		
Decreases in assets		
Increases in income		
Increases in expenses		

5 Returns, discounts and sales tax

The following topics are covered in this chapter:

- Recording sales and purchases returns
- Discounts
- Sales tax

5.1 RECORDING SALES AND PURCHASES RETURNS

LEARNING SUMMARY

After studying this section you should be able to:

- record sales and purchases returns on a cash and credit basis.

The accounting entries arising from a return from an original sale or purchase will depend upon whether the returned goods were initially on a cash or credit basis.

Sales returns

Original transaction was on a cash basis	
Dr	Sales returns
Cr	Cash

Original transaction was on a credit basis	
Dr	Sales returns
Cr	Receivables

> Sales returns may also be referred to as returns inwards.

Purchases returns

Original transaction was on a cash basis	
Dr	Cash
Cr	Purchases returns

Original transaction was on a credit basis	
Dr	Payables
Cr	Purchases returns

> Purchases returns may also be referred to as returns outwards.

5.2 DISCOUNTS

LEARNING SUMMARY

After studying this section you should be able to:

- identify the types of discounts that are available

- understand how to account for the different types of discount.

An entity may receive a discount from its suppliers – known as discount received. This is recognised as other income. An entity may give its customers a discount – known as discount allowed. This is a reduction in revenue.

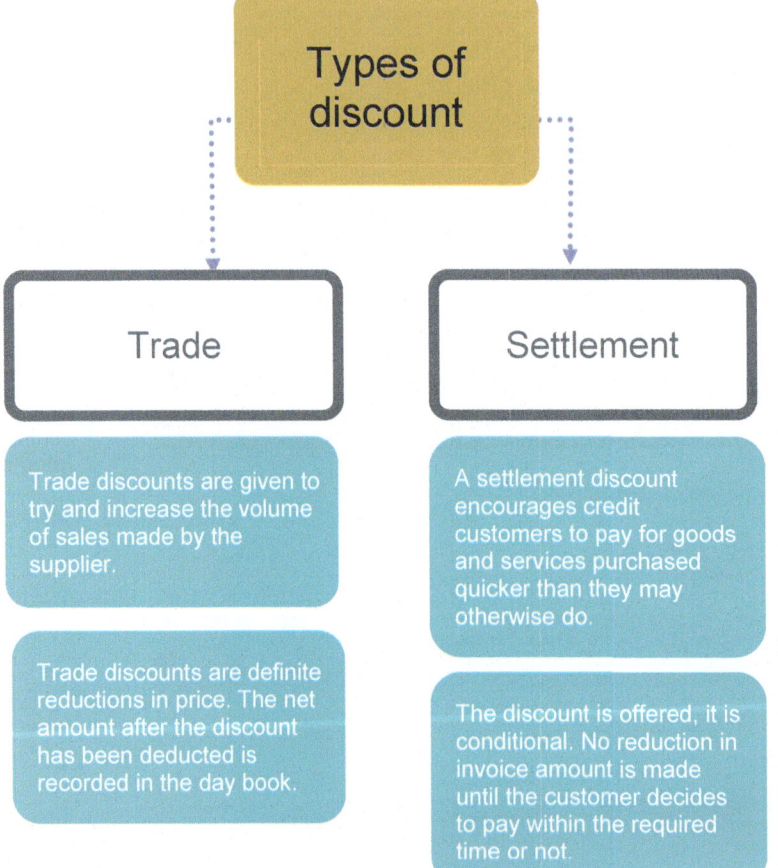

Types of discount

Trade

Trade discounts are given to try and increase the volume of sales made by the supplier.

Trade discounts are definite reductions in price. The net amount after the discount has been deducted is recorded in the day book.

Settlement

A settlement discount encourages credit customers to pay for goods and services purchased quicker than they may otherwise do.

The discount is offered, it is conditional. No reduction in invoice amount is made until the customer decides to pay within the required time or not.

A settlement discount may also be referred to as a cash or prompt payment discount.

The uncertainty of the settlement discount means the issue of variable consideration arises.

Accounting for settlement discounts

An entity should adopt one of the following approaches to deal with offering settlement discounts, depending upon whether it expects the customer to take advantage of the discount:

Prepare the sales invoice for the full amount:

If the customer is not expected to take advantage of the settlement discount offered.

Prepare the invoice for the reduced amount:

If the customer is expected to take advantage of the settlement discount. If the customer does not pay early and is no longer entitled to the discount, the full amount is due:
- The additional amount received would be treated as if it were a cash sale.
- The entity could raise a further invoice for the discount not taken.

In the assessment it should be stated whether or not the customer is expected to take the settlement discount or not.

5.3   SALES TAX

LEARNING SUMMARY

After studying this section you should be able to:

- understand the general principles of the operation of a sales tax

- calculate sales tax on transactions and record the consequent accounting entries.

DEFINITION   Sales tax is a tax imposed by the government on the supply of goods and services. Sales tax is levied at the point of sale, collected by the seller and passed on to the government or tax authority.

Sales tax is charged and paid on purchases (input tax) by suppliers and charged and collected on sales (output tax).

An entity registered for sales tax will effectively pay over the sales tax it has added to its sales and recover the sales tax it has paid on its purchases. Therefore sales tax is excluded from the reported sales and purchases of the entity.

KEY POINT Sales tax is sometimes referred to as value added tax or goods and services tax

Some entities may not be required to register to account for sales tax. 'Non-registered' entities are not allowed to add sales tax to their sales, and nor can they reclaim the sales tax on their purchases

Read questions carefully to identify whether an entity is, or is not, required to account for sales tax.

Calculation of sales tax

KEY POINT Sales tax is charged at a variety of rates around the world. It is also subject to different rates for different products within national boundaries.

ACCA will examine you on a variety of rates – the rate will always be given to you in the question.

- The net selling price is the price set by the entity that will be its sales revenue. The net amount is sales tax exclusive.

- The gross selling price is the price charged to customers. The gross amount

- The difference is the sales tax collected on behalf of the tax authority.

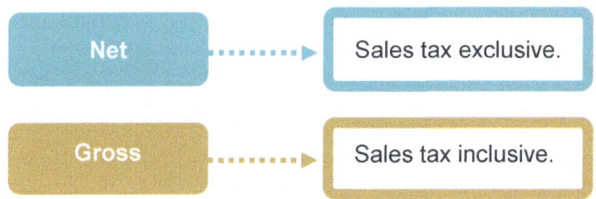

Proforma of different sales tax rates:

	20%	17.5%	15%	10%
Net selling price (tax exclusive)	100%	100%	100%	100%
Sales tax	20%	17.5%	15%	10%
Gross selling price (tax inclusive)	120%	117.5%	115%	110%

Accounting for sales tax

When making a sale	
Dr	Receivables / cash
Cr	Sales tax
Cr	Sales

When making a purchase	
Dr	Purchases
Dr	Sales tax
Cr	Payables / cash

When making a sales return	
Dr	Sales returns
Dr	Sales tax
Cr	Receivables / cash

When making a purchases return	
Dr	Payables / cash
Cr	Sales tax
Cr	Purchases returns

Sales tax control account

Typical entries in the sales tax control account are shown in the proforma below:

Sales tax control account	
Debit:	Credit:
Sales tax on purchases	Sales tax on sales
Sales tax on sales returns	Sales tax on purchases returns

> A control account is an overall summary account.

> The sales tax control account is balanced off to calculate whether an amount is owed to or by the tax authorities.

KEY POINT A balance brought down on the credit side means there is a liability owed to the tax authorities. A balance brought down on the debit side means there is an asset owed by the tax authorities and a refund is due.

Do you understand?

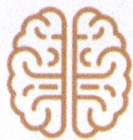

1   A discount offered for payment within a certain timescale is known as what type of discount?

2   A trade discount encourages loyalty from customers for repeat custom.

    True or false?

3   Sales tax is added onto the sales price of appropriate goods or services regardless of whether the entity is registered for sales tax or not.

    True or false?

1   Settlement discount.
2   True.
3   False. Sales tax is added onto the sales price for sales tax registered entities only.

Exam style questions

1 Jools returned unsatisfactory goods to Sandy. The goods had been sold on credit by Sandy at $100 plus sales tax of $20.

What accounting entries are required by Sandy to record the return of goods?

A Dr Purchases $100, Dr Sales tax $20, Cr Jools $120

B Dr Returns outward $100, Dr Sales tax $20, Cr Jools $120

C Dr Returns inward $100, Dr Sales tax $20, Cr Jools $120

D Dr Jools $120, Cr Returns outward $100, Cr Sales tax $20

2 **State the accounting entries required if a business made sales on credit of $10,000, on which it must account for sales tax at the rate of 20%.**

	Ledger Account:	$
Debit/Credit		
Debit/Credit		
Debit/Credit		

3 **State the accounting entries required to record the purchase of goods for resale on credit with a gross invoice value of $1,541, which includes sales tax at the rate of 15%. The business is registered to account for sales tax.**

	Ledger Account:	$
Debit/Credit		
Debit/Credit		
Debit/Credit		

4 Ella is registered for sales tax. During May, she sold goods with a list price of $600, excluding sales tax, to Kenzie on credit. As Kenzie was buying a large quantity of goods, Ella deducted trade discount of 5% of the normal list price.

If sales tax is charged at 15%, what will be the gross value of the sales invoice prepared by Ella?

$

5 In the quarter ended 31 March 20X2, Chase had taxable sales, net of sales tax, of $90,000 and taxable purchases, net of sales tax, of $72,000.

If the rate of sales tax is 10%, how much sales tax is payable to the tax authority?

A $1,800 receivable

B $2,000 receivable

C $1,800 payable

D $2,000 payable

6   A summary of the transactions of Riley, who is registered to account for sales tax at 17.5% on all transactions, shows the following for the month of August 20X9:

Outputs $60,000 (exclusive of tax)

Inputs $40,286 (inclusive of tax)

At the beginning of the period Riley owed $3,400 to the authorities, and during the period he paid $2,600 to them.

What is the amount due to the tax authorities at the end of the month?

$ [   ]

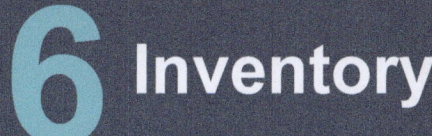

6 Inventory

The following topics are covered in this chapter:

- Year-end inventory adjustments
- Inventory in the financial statements
- Inventory valuation

6.1 YEAR-END INVENTORY ADJUSTMENTS

LEARNING SUMMARY

After studying this section you should be able to:

- record the purchase of inventory
- record opening and closing inventory.

Recording the purchase of inventory

When inventory is purchased we account for it within purchases, no adjustment is made to the inventory account until the year end:

Dr	Purchases (Statement of profit or loss)
Cr	Bank/trade payables (Statement of financial position)

You will be required to calculate inventory at the end of an accounting period and post it to the ledger system by way of a journal entry.

Accounting for closing inventory

Once the inventory has been counted and valued at the end of the accounting period, it must be included in the accounting records. The accounting adjustment is:

Dr	Inventory - Statement of financial position
Cr	Inventory - Statement of profit or loss

KEY POINT The debit entry is recording the inventory as a current asset which is shown in the statement of financial position. The credit entry is recording a reduction to the cost of sales for the goods that remain unsold.

Accounting for opening inventory

This is the balance on the inventory account, being the closing inventory figure for the previous accounting period.

No entries are put through this inventory account until the period end.

The opening inventory balance in the inventory account (debit balance) is transferred to the statement of profit or loss as part of cost of sales. The accounting adjustment is:

Dr	Inventory - Statement of profit or loss
Cr	Inventory - Statement of financial position

6.2 INVENTORY IN THE FINANCIAL STATEMENTS

LEARNING SUMMARY

After studying this section you should be able to:

- understand how inventory is recorded in the financial statements.

| Statement of financial position | ┈┈┈▶ | The closing inventory is a current asset. |

| Statement of profit or loss | ┈┈┈▶ | The cost of sales figure is made up of the opening inventory plus the purchases for the period less the closing inventory. |

6.3 INVENTORY VALUATION

LEARNING SUMMARY

After studying this section you should be able to:

- understand and apply the IASB requirements for valuing inventories

- recognise which costs should be included in valuing inventories

- calculate the value of closing inventory using FIFO (first in, first out) and AVCO (average cost) – both periodic weighted average and continuous weighted average

- understand the use of continuous and period end inventory records

- outline the disclosure requirements for inventory.

A comparison of cost and net realisable value will be required to determine which valuation is lower.

 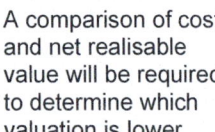

DEFINITION Cost is all expenditure incurred to bring the product or service to its present location and condition.

Cost includes the cost of purchase, material costs, import duties, freight inwards and cost of conversion.

DEFINITION Net realisable value is the actual or estimated selling price less all further costs to complete the item, less marketing, selling and distribution costs.

Methods of calculating the cost of inventory

IAS 2 Inventories outlines acceptable methods of determining cost, including specific identification (in some cases), first-in first-out (FIFO) and weighted average cost.

For inventory items that are not **interchangeable:**	Specific costs should be attributed to each individual items of inventory (unit cost).
For inventory items that are **interchangeable:**	IAS 2 permits use of the FIFO or weighted average cost methods to determine the cost of inventory.

Valuation methods

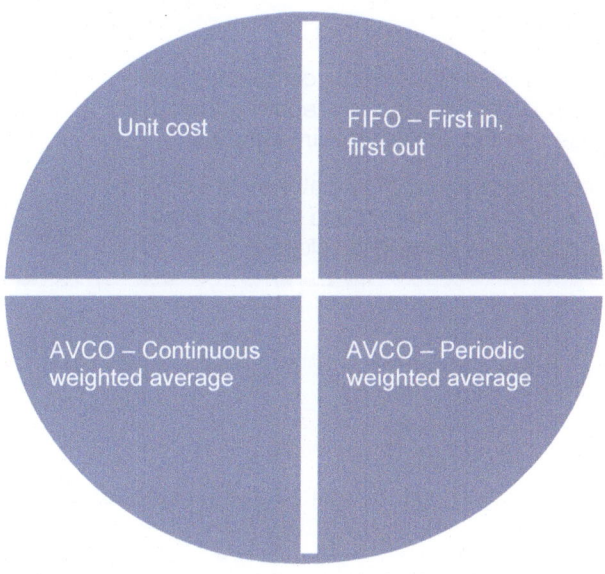

Unit cost	This is the specific cost of purchasing units of inventory.
First in first out (FIFO)	The first items of inventory received are assumed to be the first ones sold.
AVCO – periodic weighted cost	The cost of an item of inventory is calculated taking the average of all inventory held. An average cost for the period is calculated based on opening inventory + cost of inventory purchased during the year.
AVCO – continuous weighted average	The cost of an item of inventory is calculated taking the average of all inventory held. With this valuation method, an updated average cost is calculated following each a purchase of goods.

Inventory records

DEFINITION **Periodic inventory counting** is where inventory is counted and compared to inventory records at the year-end. May also be referred to as the 'period-end' method.

> **DEFINITION** **Continuous inventory counting** is where a sample of inventory items is counted at each week or month end and results of those counts are compared with the inventory records at that time. Throughout the accounting period the idea would be to count all lines of inventory at least once.

Advantages of continuous inventory counting:

- better information for inventory control

- avoiding excessive build-ups and insufficiency of different inventory lines

- less work calculating inventory at period end.

Advantages of period inventory counting:

- cheaper than the cost of maintaining continuous inventory records

- still a need to check the accuracy of the information recorded by having a physical check of some of the inventory lines.

Disclosure requirements

According to IAS 1 Presentation of Financial Statements companies are required to disclose the accounting policies adopted in preparing their financial statements, including those used to account for inventories.

IAS 2 also requires that the total carrying amount of inventories are broken down into appropriate sub-headings or classifications and that the total amount of inventory carried at net realisable value is disclosed.

Do you understand?

1   In accordance with IAS 2, inventory should be valued at the higher of cost and net realisable value.

     True or false?

2   Which of the following can be included as part of the cost of inventory?

     (i)   Cost of purchase

     (ii)   Freight costs

     (iii) Storage costs

     (iv)   Costs associated with abnormal wastage.

3   Last in first out (LIFO) is a permittable method of inventory valuation as per IAS 2.

     True or false?

4   Items of inventory have a cost of £40,000 with a realisable estimated value of £45,000 with estimated cost of realisation being £6,000. What should the inventory valuation be, in accordance with IAS 2?

     (i)   £40,000

     (ii)   £45,000

     (iii) £39,000

1   False. Inventory should be valued at the lower of cost and net realisable value.
2   (i) and (ii). Costs (iii) and (iv) are costs which should be excluded.
3   False. IAS 2 does not permit LIFO as a valid inventory valuation method.
4   (iii) The net realisable value is calculated as the estimated realisable value less the estimated costs of realisation therefore it is £39,000 which is lower than the cost of £40,000.

1   S Co sells three products – B2, S1 and L3. The following information
     was available at the year-end:

	B2	S1	L3
	$ per unit	$ per unit	$ per unit
Original cost	6	9	18
Estimated selling price	9	12	15
Selling and distribution costs	1	4	5
	units	units	units
Units in inventory	200	250	150

What was the valuation of inventory at the year-end?

$

2   A business had an opening inventory of $180,000 and a closing
     inventory of $220,000 in its financial statements for the year ended 31
     December 20X5.

     **Which of the following accounting entries are required to
     account for opening and closing inventory when preparing the
     financial statements of the business?**

		Debit	Credit
		$	$
A	Inventory account	180,000	
	Statement of P/L		180,000
	Statement P/L	220,000	
	Inventory account		220,000
B	Statement of P/L	180,000	
	Inventory account		180,000
	Inventory account	220,000	
	Statement of P/L		220,000
C	Inventory account	40,000	
	Purchases account		40,000

3 In the year ended 30 June 20X4, Elleo's records show closing inventory of 1,000 units compared to 950 units of opening inventory.

Which of the following statements is true assuming that prices have fallen throughout the year?

A   Closing inventory and profit are higher using FIFO rather than AVCO

B   Closing inventory and profit are lower using FIFO rather than AVCO

C   Closing inventory is higher and profit lower using FIFO rather than AVCO

D   Closing inventory is lower and profit higher using FIFO rather than AVCO

4 An item of inventory was purchased for $500. It is expected to be sold for $1,200 although $250 will need to be spent on it in order to achieve the sale. To replace the same item of inventory would cost $650.

At what value should this item of inventory be included in the financial statements?

$ _____

7 Non-current assets – acquisition and depreciation

The following topics are covered in this chapter:

- Classifying capital and revenue expenditure
- Non-current assets
- Depreciation
- Non-current assets register

7.1 CLASSIFYING CAPITAL AND REVENUE EXPENDITURE

LEARNING SUMMARY

After studying this section you should be able to:

- explain the difference between capital and revenue items.

DEFINITION   Capital expenditure is expenditure likely to increase the future earning capability of the entity.

DEFINITION   Revenue expenditure is expenditure associated with maintaining the entity's present earning capability.

Capital expenditure

Acquisition of non-current assets acquired for use in the business, not for resale.

Expenditure on existing non-current assets aimed at increasing their earning capacity.

Revenue expenditure

Expenditure relevant to the running of the business i.e. administration costs.

Expenditure on current assets i.e. inventory.

Expenditure on maintaining the earning capacity of non-current assets e.g. repairs and renewals.

KEY POINT Capital expenditure is expenditure the business intends to receive the benefits of over a long period of time. Revenue expenditure relates to generating revenue in the current accounting period.

7.2 NON-CURRENT ASSETS

LEARNING SUMMARY

After studying this section you should be able to:

- define non-current assets, recognising the differences from current assets and outlining how non-current asset balances are disclosed on the financial statements

- prepare ledger entries to record the acquisition of non-current assets

- classify expenditure as capital or revenue expenditure.

Non-current assets are resources acquired by an entity with the intended use of earning revenue for more than one accounting period.

Non-current assets:

- are not normally acquired for resale

- can be either tangible or intangible

- are used to generate income directly or indirectly for a business entity

- are not normally liquid assets (i.e. not easily and quickly converted into cash without a significant loss in value).

Accounting for non-current assets

Dr	Non-current asset – cost (SoFP)
Cr	Bank/cash/payables (SoFP)

> The credit entry depends on the method of payment for the non-current asset.

> **KEY POINT** The cost of the non-current asset includes the amounts incurred to acquire the asset and bring it to a working condition.

According to IAS 16 Property Plant and Equipment, cost consists of, or excludes, the following elements:

Includes:	Excludes:	
capital expenditure:	revenue expenditure:	
purchase price	repairs	
delivery costs	renewals	
legal fees	repainting	
subsequent expenditure which enhances the asset	administration	
trials and tests	general overheads	
	training costs	
	waste	

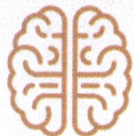

Do you understand?

1   Classify each of the following items of expenditure as either capital or revenue expenditure.

   (i)   Repainting of a building

   (ii)   Installation of a new central heating system

   (iii) Repairs on a delivery van

   (iv)   Providing drainage for a new piece of water-extraction equipment.

2   Revenue expenditure is expenditure relating to the acquisition or improvement of non-current assets.
     True or false?

3   A business entity buys an item of machinery for long-term use. Which of the following is NOT capital expenditure?

   (i)   The purchase price of $1,000

   (ii)   Delivery fees of $125

   (iii) $250 spent on training employees to use the machine

   (iv) $300 incurred on testing the machine.

7.3   DEPRECIATION

LEARNING SUMMARY

After studying this section you should be able to:

- understand and explain the purpose of depreciation.

- calculate the charge for depreciation using straight line and reducing balance methods

- Identify the circumstances where different methods of depreciation would be appropriate

- account for depreciation expense and accumulated depreciation and record depreciation in the financial statements.

DEFINITION   Depreciation is 'the systematic allocation of the depreciable amount of an asset over its useful life' (IAS 16 para 6).

KEY POINT To calculate depreciation there are three factors to consider; the cost of the asset, the useful economic life and the residual value.

Cost	Amount capitalised.
Useful economic life	Period over which economic benefits are expected to be derived from the asset.
Residual value	Amount that the asset is expected to be sold for at the end of its useful economic life.

Methods of depreciation

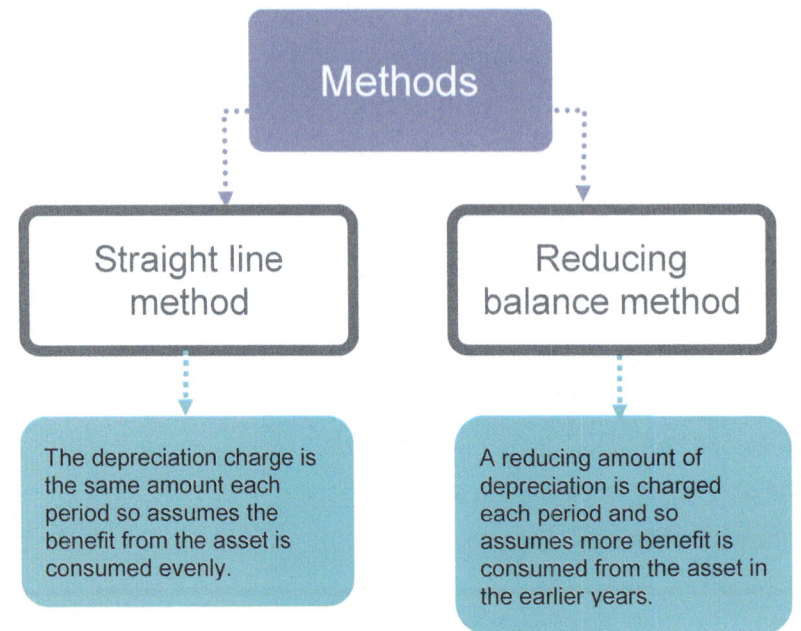

Methods

Straight line method

Reducing balance method

The depreciation charge is the same amount each period so assumes the benefit from the asset is consumed evenly.

A reducing amount of depreciation is charged each period and so assumes more benefit is consumed from the asset in the earlier years.

Note the two common types of depreciation and in what circumstances each is suitable.

Straight line method of depreciation

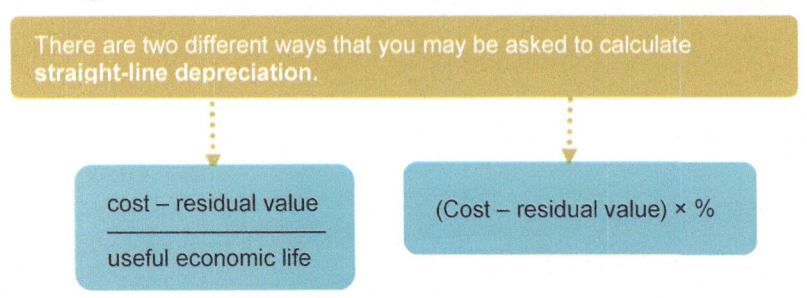

There are two different ways that you may be asked to calculate **straight-line depreciation.**

$$\frac{\text{cost} - \text{residual value}}{\text{useful economic life}}$$

$$(\text{Cost} - \text{residual value}) \times \%$$

Depending on what information is provided in a question the formula or percentage method can be used.

Reducing balance method of depreciation

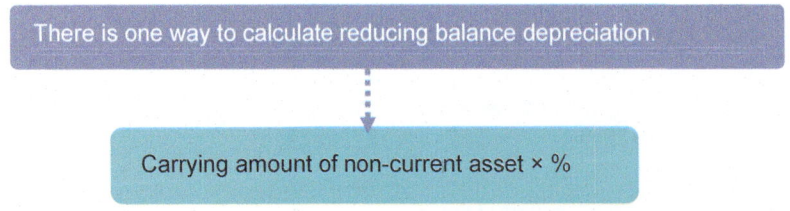

There is one way to calculate reducing balance depreciation.

Carrying amount of non-current asset × %

KEY POINT Carrying amount = original cost of the non-current asset less accumulated depreciation for the asset to date.

Accounting for depreciation

Dr	Depreciation expense (SPL)
Cr	Non-current asset – accumulated depreciation (SoFP)

KEY POINT The depreciation expense is a profit or loss account and therefore is not accumulated.

The accumulated depreciation account is a statement of financial position account and as the name suggests is accumulated, i.e. reflects all depreciation to date. On the statement of financial position the non-current assets would be analysed into the cost, accumulated depreciation to date and the consequent carrying amount.

> The carrying amount of a non-current asset may also be referred to as the carrying value.

Assets bought or sold during an accounting period

If a non-current asset is bought or sold in the period, there are two ways in which the depreciation could be accounted for:

- provide a full year's depreciation in the year of acquisition and none in the year of disposal.

- monthly or pro-rata depreciation based on the exact number of months that the asset has been owned.

Changing estimates

The same rates and methods of depreciation should be applied consistently throughout the life of their business. However, if the estimates of useful life and/or residual value are believed to be inappropriate a change is permitted. A new depreciation charge of the asset based on the revised estimate of useful life or residual value is calculated.

7.4 NON-CURRENT ASSETS REGISTER

LEARNING SUMMARY

After studying this section you should be able to:

- explain the purpose and function of an asset register .

A non-current assets register is a record of the non-current assets held by a business. It forms part of the internal control system of an organisation.

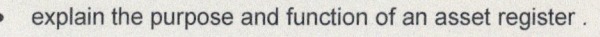

Contents of a non-current assets register:	
cost	location of asset
date of purchase	depreciation method
description of asset	expected useful life
serial/reference number	carrying amount

Do you understand?

A non-current asset was purchased by Bob on 1 January 20X1 for $48,000. It has an estimated useful economic life of 6 years and an estimated residual value of $8,500.

What would be the depreciation charge for this asset for the year ending 31 December 20X3 using:

1   straight line depreciation

2   reducing balance depreciation at 25% per annum?

	$
Cost	48,000
Depreciation to 31 Dec 20X1 (48,000 × 25%)	(12,000)
Carrying amount at 31 Dec 20X1	36,000
Depreciation to 31 Dec 20X2 (36,000 × 25%)	(9,000)
Carrying amount at 31 Dec 20X2	27,000
Depreciation to 31 Dec 20X3 (27,000 × 25%)	(6,750)
	20,250
Depreciation for the year ended 31 December 20X3	**$6,750**

1   ($48,000 - $8,500) / 6 = $6,583

2    $6,750

1   W Co bought a new printing machine from abroad. The cost of the machine was $80,000. The installation costs were $5,000 and the employees received training on how to use the machine, at a cost of $2,000. Before using the machine to print customers' orders, pre-production safety testing was undertaken at a cost of $1,000.

What should be the cost of the machine in W Co's statement of financial position?

$ [   ]

2   **Which one of the following items should be accounted for as capital expenditure?**

A   The cost of painting a building

B   The replacement of broken windows in a building

C   The purchase of a car by a car dealer for re-sale

D   Legal fees incurred on the purchase of a building

3   **Which of the following statements best describes depreciation?**

A   It is a means of spreading the payment for non-current assets over a period of years.

B   It is a decline in the market value of the assets.

C   It is a means of spreading the net cost of non-current assets over their estimated useful life.

D   It is a means of estimating the amount of money needed to replace the assets.

4   **The reducing balance method of depreciating non-current assets is more appropriate than the straight-line method when:**

A   there is no expected residual value for the asset

B   the expected life of the asset is not capable of being estimated

C   the asset is expected to be replaced in a short period of time

D   the asset decreases in value less in later years than in the early years of use

8 Non-current assets – disposal and revaluation

The following topics are covered in this chapter:

- Disposal of non-current assets
- Revaluation of non-current assets
- Depreciation and disposal of a revalued asset
- Disclosure requirements

8.1 DISPOSAL OF NON-CURRENT ASSETS

LEARNING SUMMARY

After studying this section you should be able to:

- understand which balances need to be removed on disposal
- calculate whether a profit or loss has been made on disposal, including part exchange transactions
- prepare ledger entries to record the disposal of non-current assets.

Removal of existing ledger account balances

When a non-current asset is disposed of (i.e. sold or scrapped), there are balances in the ledger accounts that relate to this asset that need to be removed. These balances are:

- the original cost of the non-current asset
- the accumulated depreciation relating to the non-current asset

To remove these balances a disposals ledger account is opened.

KEY POINT The disposals account is a profit or loss account.

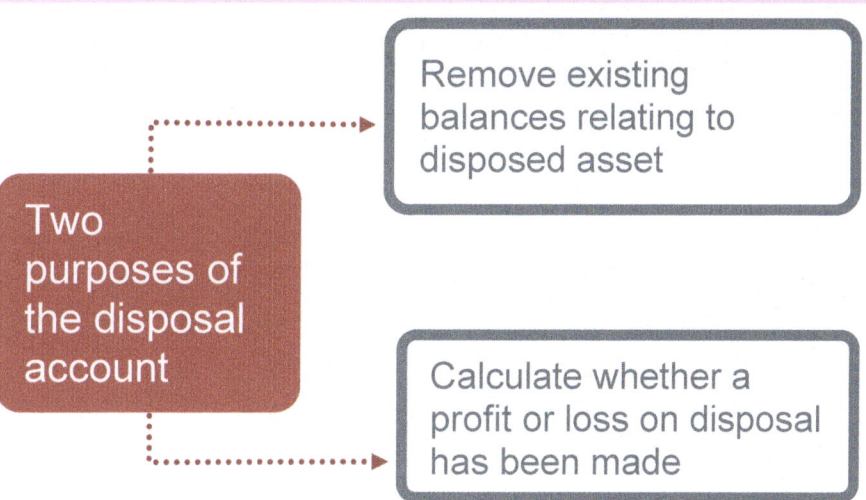

Two purposes of the disposal account → Remove existing balances relating to disposed asset

Two purposes of the disposal account → Calculate whether a profit or loss on disposal has been made

Calculating a profit or loss on disposal

When a non-current asset is disposed of (i.e. sold or scrapped), it is unlikely that the proceeds from sale will be equal to the carrying amount of the asset in the statement of financial position.

The difference between the carrying amount and the sale proceeds will be either a profit or a loss on the disposal of a non-current asset.

Profit on disposal	this will occur where the sales proceeds exceed the carrying amount
Loss on disposal	this will occur where the sales proceeds are lower than the carrying amount

Steps to dispose of a non-current asset

Step 1

Remove the original cost of the non-current asset from the 'noncurrent asset' account.

Dr	Disposals account
Cr	NC assets cost account

Step 2

Remove the original cost of the non-current asset from the 'noncurrent asset' account.

Dr	Accumulated depreciation account
Cr	Disposals account

Step 3

Record the proceeds.

Dr	Cash account
Cr	Disposals account

If there are no proceeds step 3 is not required.

KEY POINT The balance on the disposal account is the profit or loss on disposal.

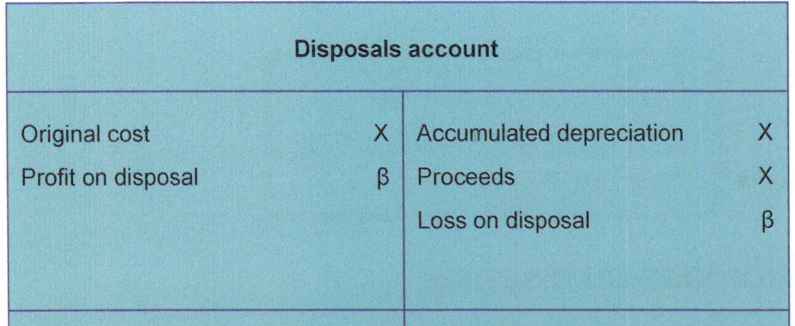

Disposals account				
Original cost	X	Accumulated depreciation	X
Profit on disposal	β	Proceeds	X
		Loss on disposal	β
	X		X

Remember the profit or loss on disposal can be calculated by comparing the proceeds to the carrying amount.

Disposal through a part exchange agreement

A part exchange agreement arises where an old asset is provided in part payment for a new one, the balance of the new asset being paid in cash.

Note that steps 1 & 2 are identical to those of a cash disposal.

Step 1	
Remove the original cost of the non-current asset from the 'noncurrent asset' account.	
Dr	Disposals account
Cr	NC assets cost account

Step 2	
Remove the original cost of the non-current asset from the 'noncurrent asset' account.	
Dr	Accumulated depreciation account
Cr	Disposals account

Step 3	
Record the part exchange allowance.	
Dr	NC assets cost account
Cr	Disposals account

Step 3 - The debit entry to the NC assets cost account is recording part of the cost of the new asset. The credit entry records the proceeds from the old asset.

Step 4	
Record the cash paid for the new asset.	
Dr	NC assets cost account
Cr	Cash account

The profit or loss on disposal for a part-exchange can be calculated by comparing the part exchange allowance to the carrying amount.

KEY POINT The balance on the disposal account is the profit or loss on disposal.

8.2 REVALUATION OF NON-CURRENT ASSETS

LEARNING SUMMARY

After studying this section you should be able to:

- record the revaluation of a non-current asset

According to IAS 16, items of property, plant and equipment can be measured and accounted for using the revaluation model.

KEY POINT Revaluation surplus = Revalued amount – Carrying amount.

Revaluation for a non-depreciated asset

Dr	Non-current asset cost account
Cr	Revaluation surplus

The amount of the increase in value is the revaluation surplus.

Revaluation for a depreciated asset

Dr	Accumulated depreciation account
Dr	Non-current asset cost account
Cr	Revaluation surplus

The accumulated depreciation is debited with the accumulated depreciation to date on the asset.

The non-current asset cost account is debited with the difference between the original cost and the revalued amount.

The revaluation surplus is credited with the difference between the carrying amount and the revalued amount.

The revaluation gain for the year is disclosed on the face of the statement of profit or loss and other comprehensive income as an item of 'other comprehensive income'. This amount is added to any earlier revaluation from a previous accounting period to arrive at a cumulative revaluation surplus in the statement of changes in equity (SOCIE) and statement of financial position.

8.3 DEPRECIATION AND DISPOSAL OF A REVALUED ASSET

LEARNING SUMMARY

After studying this section you should be able to:

- calculate depreciation on a revalued non-current asset including the transfer of excess depreciation between the revaluation surplus and retained earnings

- understand how to account for the disposal of a revalued asset.

Depreciation of a revalued asset

KEY POINT When a non-current asset has been revalued, the charge for depreciation should be based on the revalued amount and the remaining useful life of the asset.

This charge will be higher than depreciation prior to the revaluation and will be charged to profit or loss as normal.

The excess of the new annual depreciation charge over the old depreciation charge may be the subject of an annual transfer from revaluation surplus to retained earnings (within the equity section of the statement of financial position) as follows:

Dr	Revaluation surplus
Cr	Retained earnings

The transfer of the excess depreciation is a choice made by the business. It is not compulsory.

Disposal of a revalued asset

The disposal of a revalued asset is recorded as normal, with the asset and accumulated depreciation amounts cleared to a disposal account so that a gain or loss on disposal can be calculated.

The accounting entry for this is:

Dr	Revaluation surplus
Cr	Retained earnings

8.4   DISCLOSURE REQUIREMENTS

LEARNING SUMMARY

After studying this section you should be able to:

- outline the disclosure requirements.

Statement of financial position	┄┄►	The aggregate of the carrying amounts of the non-current assets disclosed on the statement of financial position.
Statement of profit or loss	┄┄►	Depreciation charge included within the relevant expense categories.
Notes to the accounts	┄┄►	• Disclosure of depreciation methods and rates used. • Non-current assets disclosure. • Details of revaluations.

According to IAS 16 Property Plant and Equipment, there are a number of disclosure requirements relating to non-current assets.

The principal disclosure requirements include:

- The measurement bases used for arriving at the carrying amount of the asset (e.g. cost or valuation). If more than one basis has been used, the amounts for each basis must be disclosed.

- Depreciation methods used, with details of useful lives or the depreciation rates used.

- The gross amount of each asset heading and its related accumulated depreciation (aggregated with accumulated impairment losses) at the beginning and end of the period.

- A reconciliation of the carrying amount at the beginning and end of the period, showing:

  – additions

  – assets classified as held for sale

  – disposals

  – revaluations

  – depreciation.

Do you understand?

1   A non-current asset had a carrying amount of $1,228.80 and was disposed of for proceeds of $1,200.

The result of this was:

(i)   a loss on disposal of $240.00

(ii)   a loss on disposal of $28.80

(iii)   a profit on disposal of $28.80

(iv)   a profit on disposal of $240.00

2   When a non-current asset has been revalued, the charge for depreciation should be based on the revalued amount and the remaining useful life of the asset.

True or false?

3   A loss on disposal occurs where the sales proceeds exceed the carrying amount.

True or false?

1   (ii) A loss on disposal of $28.80 occurs as the proceeds are lower than the carrying amount by $28.80.
2   True.
3   False. A profit on disposal occurs where the sales proceeds exceed the carrying amount.

1   The non-current asset register shows a carrying amount for non-current assets of $85,600; the ledger accounts include a cost balance of $185,000 and an accumulated depreciation balance of $55,000.

Which one of the following statements may explain the discrepancy?

A   The omission of an addition of land costing $30,000 from the ledger account and the omission of the disposal of an asset from the register (cost $25,600 and accumulated depreciation at disposal $11,200).

B   The omission of the revaluation of an asset upwards by $16,600 and the depreciation charge of $20,000 from the ledger account and the omission of the disposal of an asset with a carrying amount of $41,000 from the register.

C   The omission of the disposal of an asset from the ledger accounts (cost $25,600 and accumulated depreciation at disposal $11,200) and the omission of an addition of land costing $30,000 from the register.

D   The omission of an upwards revaluation by $16,400 from the register and the accidental debiting of the depreciation charge of $28,000 to the accumulated depreciation ledger account.

2   Louisa bought an asset on the 1st January 20X4 for $235,000. He has depreciated it at 30% using the reducing balance method. On 1st January 20X7, Louisa revalued the asset to $300,000.

What accounting entries should Louisa post to record the revaluation?

A   Dr Non-current assets – cost $65,000

Dr Accumulated depreciation $154,395

Cr Revaluation surplus $219,395

B   Dr Non-current assets – cost $65,000

Dr Accumulated depreciation $211,500

Cr Revaluation surplus $276,500

C   Dr Revaluation surplus $219,395

Cr Non-current assets – cost $65,000

Cr Accumulated depreciation $154,395

D   Dr Revaluation surplus $276,500

Cr Non-current assets – cost $65,000

Cr Accumulated depreciation $211,500

Which one of the following statements is true in relation to the non-current asset register?

A   It is an alternative name for the non-current asset ledger account.

B   It is a list of the physical non-current assets rather than their financial cost.

C   It is a schedule of planned maintenance of non-current assets for use by the plant engineer.

D   It is a schedule of the cost and other information about each individual non-current asset.

4   The plant and equipment account in the records of C Co for the year ended 31 December 20X6 is shown below:

Plant and equipment – cost

	$		$
Balance b/f	960,000		
1 July Cash	48,000	30 Sept Disposals	84,000
		Balance c/f	924,000
	1,008,000		1,008,000

C Co's policy is to charge straight line depreciation at 20% per year on a pro rata basis.

What should be the charge for depreciation in C Co's statement of profit or loss for the year ended 31 December 20X6?

$ [   ]

9.1 INTANGIBLE ASSETS

LEARNING SUMMARY

After studying this section you should be able to:

- recognise the difference between tangible and intangible non-current assets
- identify types of intangible assets
- explain the purpose of amortisation.

DEFINITION An **intangible asset** is 'an identifiable non-monetary asset without physical substance' (IAS 38, para 8).

Intangible assets can be purchased or internally generated, e.g. brand names.

KEY POINT As a general rule, purchased intangible assets are capitalised whereas internally generated intangible assets are not recognised in the financial statements.

- When the cost and expected useful life of an intangible asset can be reliably measured, they must be amortised to reflect the using up or wearing out of that asset.

- If the expected useful life cannot be reliably estimated, the intangible asset is subject to an annual impairment review, rather than an annual amortisation charge.

> Amortisation is really the same as depreciation but a term used in relation to intangible assets.

> Impairment is a reduction in the recoverable amount of a non-current asset below its book value.

Goodwill

Trademarks

Development costs

Examples of intangible assets

Licences

Brands

Copyrights

Recognition of intangible assets

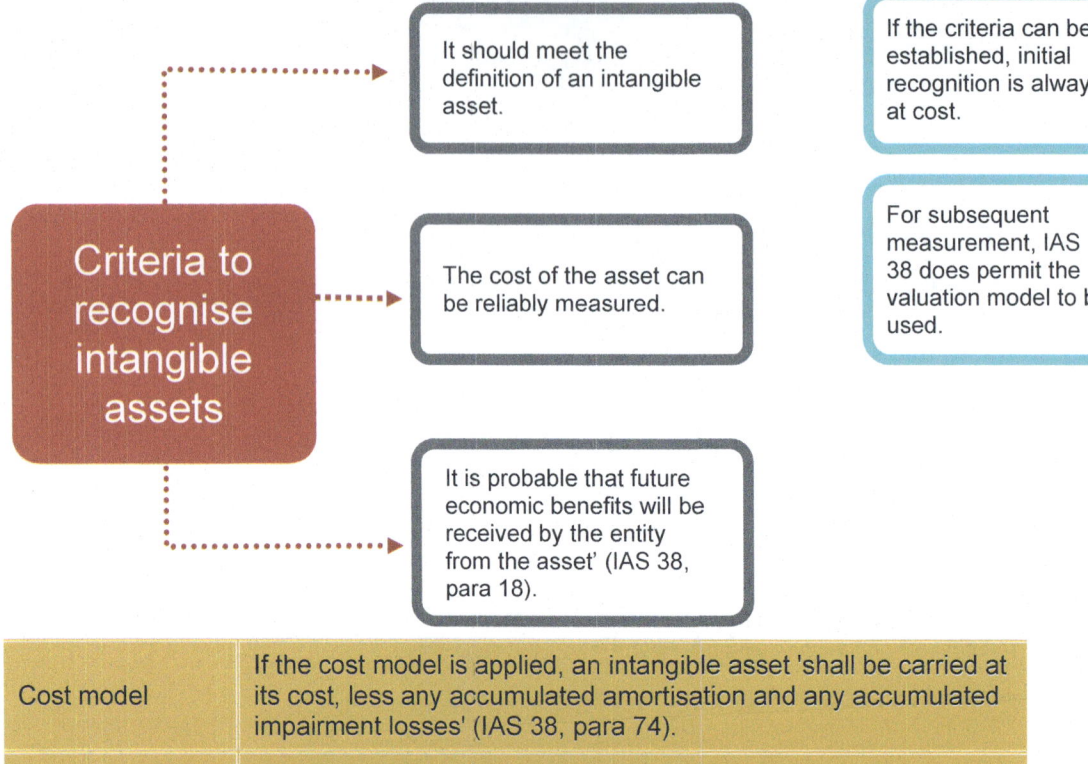

Cost model	If the cost model is applied, an intangible asset 'shall be carried at its cost, less any accumulated amortisation and any accumulated impairment losses' (IAS 38, para 74).
Valuation model	For the valuation model to be applied, 'fair value should be measured by reference to an active market' (IAS 38, para 75).

9.2 RESEARCH AND DEVELOPMENT

LEARNING SUMMARY

After studying this section you should be able to:

- identify the definition and treatment of 'research costs' and 'development costs' in accordance with International Financial Reporting Standards.

DEFINITION   Research is 'original and planned investigation undertaken with the prospect of gaining new scientific or technical knowledge and understanding' (IAS 38, para 8).

Accounting treatment of research expenditure:

KEY POINT All research expenditure must be written off to the statement of profit or loss as it is incurred.

DEFINITION   Development is 'the application of research findings or other knowledge to a plan or design for the production of new or substantially improved materials, devices, products, processes, systems or services before the start of commercial production or use' (IAS 38, para 8).

KEY POINT Development costs are a particular class of research expenditure that meets certain criteria and which therefore enables a separate accounting treatment to be applied to it.

Accounting treatment of development expenditure:

Development costs must be capitalised as an intangible asset on the statement of financial position provided that all of the following criteria are met:

S	········▶	separate project
E	········▶	expenditure identifiable and reliably measured
C	········▶	commercially viable
T	········▶	technically feasible
O	········▶	overall profitable
R	········▶	resources available to complete

If the 'SECTOR' criteria are not met, development expenditure is treated as research activity.

KEY POINT Each project should be reviewed at the year-end to ensure that the 'SECTOR' criteria are still met. If they are no longer met, the previously capitalised expenditure must be written off to the statement of profit or loss immediately.

9.3 DISCLOSURE REQUIREMENTS

LEARNING SUMMARY

After studying this section you should be able to:

- outline the disclosure requirements.

The financial statements should disclose:

- the amortisation method used and the expected period of amortisation

- a reconciliation of the carrying amounts at the beginning and end of the period, showing new expenditure incurred, amortisation and amounts written off because a project no longer qualifies for capitalisation, and

- amortisation charged during the period.

The financial statements should also disclose the total amount of research and development expenditure recognised as an expense during the period.

Do you understand?

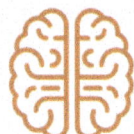

1. Categorise the following non-current assets as tangible or intangible:
   (i) Land & buildings
   (ii) Motor vehicles
   (iii) Patents
   (iv) Licences.

2. Goodwill is most appropriately classified as a tangible non-current asset.

   True or false?

3. RD Ltd has spent $100,000 investigating a chemical compound, known as ZZ23R and has found it is not harmful to mammals. Should this be classified as development costs?

4. Drake Ltd has incurred a further $250,000 using a specialised gel for creating prototypes of a new heat-resistant suit for stuntmen. Should this be classified as development costs?

1. (i) and (ii) are tangible non-current assets, (iii) and (iv) are intangible assets.
2. False. Goodwill is most appropriately classified as an intangible non-current asset.
3. No – this should not be classified as development as it has no form of commercial production in mind.
4. Yes – this should be classified as development as it has commercial production in mind.

1   Which one of the following statements is correct?

A   If all the conditions specified in IAS 38 Intangible assets are met, the directors can chose whether to capitalise the development expenditure or not.

B   Amortisation of capitalised development expenditure will appear as an item in an entity's statement of changes in equity.

C   Capitalised development costs are shown in the statement of financial position as non-current assets.

D   Capitalised development expenditure must be amortised over a period not exceeding five years.

2   What is the correct accounting treatment for an intangible asset with an indefinite useful life?

A   It is recognised at cost for as long as the entity has the intangible asset.

B   It is recognised at cost and is subject to an annual impairment review.

C   It is recognised at cost and the entity must make an estimate of estimated useful life so that it can be amortised.

D   It cannot be recognised as an intangible asset as it would not be possible to calculate an annual amortisation charge.

3   Which one of the following statements best defines an intangible asset?

A   An intangible asset is an asset with no physical substance

B   An intangible asset is always generated internally by a business

C   An intangible asset is an asset which cannot be sold

D   An intangible asset is a purchased asset which has no physical substance

4   Which THREE of the following statements are correct in relation to application of IAS 38 Intangible Assets?

A   Research costs should be expensed to the statement of profit or loss.

B   All types of goodwill can be capitalised.

C   Capitalised development costs that no longer meet the criteria specified by IAS 38 must be written off to the statement of profit or loss.

D   Capitalised development costs are amortised from the date the assets is available to use or sell.

E   Research costs written off can be re-capitalised when the developed asset is feasible.

F   Only purchased intangibles can be capitalised.

10 Accruals and prepayments

The following topics are covered in this chapter:

- Accruals basis of accounting
- Accrued expenditure
- Prepaid expenditure
- Accrued income
- Prepaid income

10.1 ACCRUALS BASIS OF ACCOUNTING

LEARNING SUMMARY

After studying this section you should be able to:

- understand how the accruals (matching) concept applies to accruals and prepayments.

KEY POINT The accruals concept requires recording revenues when they are earned and not when they are received in cash, and recording expenses when they are incurred and not when they are paid.

To calculate the profit for the period, all the income and expenditure relating to the period must be included, whether or not the cash has been received or paid or an invoice received.

 =

| Profit | Income earned | Expenditure incurred |

10.2 ACCRUED EXPENDITURE

LEARNING SUMMARY

After studying this section you should be able to:

- define and account for accrued expenditure.

DEFINITION An **accrual** arises where expenses of the business, relating to the year, have not been paid by the year end.

The expense relevant to the year should be recognised and a corresponding statement of financial position liability – an accrual.

| Dr | Expense account (Statement of profit or loss) |
| Cr | Accrual (Statement of financial position) |

KEY POINT Accrued expenses reduce profit in the statement of profit or loss.

10.3 PREPAID EXPENDITURE

DEFINITION A **prepayment** arises where some of the following year's expenses have been paid in the current year.

The part of the expense which is not relevant to this year should not be recognised in the current period and a corresponding statement of financial position asset should be created - a prepayment.

Dr	Prepayment (Statement of financial position)
Cr	Expense account (Statement of profit or loss)

KEY POINT Prepaid expenses increase profit in the statement of profit or loss.

10.4 ACCRUED INCOME

DEFINITION Accrued income arises where income has been earned in the accounting period but has not yet been received.

The income earned but not recognised in the statement of profit needs to be recorded and a corresponding asset in the statement of financial position - accrued income needs to be created.

Dr	Accrued income (Statement of financial position)
Cr	Income (Statement of profit or loss)

KEY POINT Accrued income creates additional income on the statement of profit or loss, and so increases overall profits.

10.5 PREPAID INCOME

DEFINITION Prepaid income arises where income has been received in the accounting period but which relates to the next accounting period.

The income not relating to the year from the statement of profit or loss should be removed and a corresponding liability in the statement of financial position - prepaid income should be created.

Dr	Income (Statement of profit or loss)
Cr	Prepaid income (Statement of financial position)

KEY POINT Prepaid income reduces income in the statement of profit or loss and hence reduces overall profits.

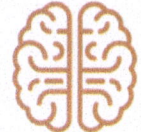

Do you understand?

1   Which of the following statements is false?

   (i)   Accruals decrease profit

   (ii)   Accrued income decreases profit

   (iii) A prepayment is an asset

   (iv)   An accrual is a liability

2   The accruals concept implies that the profits must be charged with expenses incurred, irrespective of whether or not an invoice has been received.

   True or false?

3   Accrued income arises where income has been received in the accounting period but which relates to the next accounting period.

   True or false?

1   (ii) Accrued income is income not yet received when the service has been provided. When the adjustment is made to recognise accrued income it will increase profit.
2   True
3   False this definition is referring to prepaid income. Accrued income arises where income has been earned in the accounting period but has not yet been received.

Exam style questions

1 Fraser's year-end is 30 September. On 1 January 20X9 Fraser took out a loan of $100,000 with annual interest of 12%. The interest is payable in equal instalments on the first day of April, July, October and January in arrears.

How much should be charged to the statement of profit or loss account for the year ended 30 September 20X9, and how much should be accrued on the statement of financial position?

A	Statement of profit or loss	$12,000
	Statement of financial position	$3,000
B	Statement of profit or loss	$9,000
	Statement of financial position	$3,000
C	Statement of profit or loss	$9,000
	Statement of financial position	$0
D	Statement of profit or loss	$6,000
	Statement of financial position	$3,000

2 Lamb Ltd sublets part of its office accommodation to earn rental income.

The rent is received quarterly in advance on 1 January, 1 April, 1 July and 1 October. The annual rent has been $24,000 for some years, but it was increased to $30,000 from 1 July 20X5.

What amounts for rent should appear in Lamb Ltd's financial statements for the year ended 31 January 20X6?

A	Statement of profit or loss	$27,500
	Statement of financial position	$5,000 in accrued income
B	Statement of profit or loss	$27,000
	Statement of financial position	$2,500 in accrued income
C	Statement of profit or loss	$27,000
	Statement of financial position	$2,500 in prepaid income
D	Statement of profit or loss	$27,500
	Statement of financial position	$5,000 in prepaid income

3 At 1 September, the motor expenses account showed 4 months' insurance prepaid of $80 and fuel costs accrued of $95.

During September, the outstanding fuel bill was paid, plus further bills of $245. At 30 September there was a further outstanding fuel bill of $120.

What was the expense included in the statement of profit or loss for motor expenses for September?

11 Receivables

The following topics are covered in this chapter:
- Cash and credit sales
- Irrecoverable debts
- Allowances for receivables

11.1 CASH AND CREDIT SALES

LEARNING SUMMARY

After studying this section you should be able to:

- account for cash and credit sales
- understand the purpose of an aged receivable analysis
- understand the purpose of a credit limit.

Accounting for cash and credit sales

If a sale is for cash, the customer pays for the goods/services at the point of sale:

Dr	Cash
Cr	Sales revenue

If the sale is on credit, the customer will pay for the goods or services after receiving them. Trading terms typically allow customers 30 – 60 days when purchasing goods and services on credit.

KEY POINT Under the accruals concept, the sale is recorded in the ledger accounts when the right to the income is earned.

The right to the income being earned is usually the point at which the goods or services are delivered.

Dr	Receivables
Cr	Sales revenue

The balance on the receivables account is cleared when the credit customer pays their debt.

Dr	Cash
Cr	Receivables

Aged receivable analysis

DEFINITION An **aged receivables analysis** is usually a list, ordered by name, showing how much each customer owes and how old their debts are.

The credit control function of a business uses the aged receivable analysis to keep track of outstanding debts and chase any that are overdue.

KEY POINT Timely collection of debts improves cash flow and reduces the risk of them becoming irrecoverable.

Credit limits

The advantages of setting credit limits as part of the credit control strategy:

- reduce the risk to the businesses of irrecoverable debts by limiting the amount sold on credit

- help build up the trust of a new customer.

11.2 IRRECOVERABLE DEBTS

LEARNING SUMMARY

After studying this section you should be able to:

- prepare the bookkeeping entries to write off a irrecoverable debt

- record an irrecoverable debt recovered

- identify the impact of irrecoverable debts on the statement of profit or loss and on the statement of financial position.

KEY POINT It is prudent to remove irrecoverable debts from the accounts and to charge the amount as an expense to the statement of profit or loss.

Dr	Irrecoverable debts expense
Cr	Receivables

Whilst the debit entry increases the expenses on the statement of profit or loss, the credit to the receivables reduces the value of the assets on the statement of financial position.

Recovery of irrecoverable debts

A debt may be written off as irrecoverable in one accounting period, and the money, or part of the money, due is then unexpectedly received in a subsequent accounting period.

Dr	Cash
Cr	Irrecoverable debts expense

11.3 ALLOWANCES FOR RECIEVABLES

LEARNING SUMMARY

After studying this section you should be able to:

- prepare the bookkeeping entries to create and adjust an allowance for receivables.

There may be some debts in the accounts where there is some cause for concern but they are not yet definitely irrecoverable.

> **DEFINITION** An **allowance for receivables** is made where there is doubt about the recovery of a debt.

> Under the prudence concept, revenue should not be overestimated and expenses should not be underestimated.

If this is the case it is not be appropriate to eliminate the receivable balance as the credit customer may still pay. However, we recognise that the balance on the receivables account is probably less than it appears to be, this is in line with the prudence concept.

Dr	Irrecoverable debts expense
Cr	Allowance for receivables

A doubtful debt that becomes irrecoverable

When a debt is written off as irrecoverable, the transaction is treated the same as for an irrecoverable debt write off:

Dr	Irrecoverable debts expense
Cr	Receivables

Any subsequent change to the allowance for receivables should be dealt with as a separate matter.

Increases and decreases to the allowance for receivables

> **KEY POINT** If there is already an allowance for receivables in the accounts (opening allowance); only the movement in the allowance is charged to the statement of profit or loss (closing allowance less opening allowance).

To increase the allowance for receivables	
Dr	Irrecoverable debts expense
Cr	Allowance for receivables
To decrease the allowance for receivables	
Dr	Allowance for receivables
Cr	Irrecoverable debts expense

When calculating and accounting for a movement in the allowance for receivables, the following steps should be taken:	
Step 1:	Write off irrecoverable debts.
Step 2:	Calculate the receivables balance as adjusted for the write-offs.
Step 3:	Ascertain the allowance for receivables required.
Step 4:	Compare to the brought forward allowance.
Step 5:	Account for the change in allowance to determine the expense or credit to the statement of profit or loss.
Step 6:	In the financial statements, deduct the closing allowance for receivables from the receivables balance.

Do you understand?

1   Under what circumstance would an irrecoverable debt be recognised?

2   Under what circumstance would an allowance for receivables be made?

3   At 1 July 20X2 there was a balance on a business's allowance for doubtful debts account of £4,300. At 30 June 20X3 the business had receivables of £120,000 although £2,500 of these are to be written off as irrecoverable debts. There is to be a general allowance against doubtful debts of 4% at the year end.

Draft the journal entry required to account for the irrecoverable debts and allowance for receivables.

1   An irrecoverable debt would be recognised when information comes to light to suggest that a customer is unwilling or unable to pay their debt in full.

2   An allowance for receivables would be recognised when there is some doubt as to whether some of the entity's receivables may fail to pay their debts in full.

3   Allowance for receivables required:

	$
($120,000 – $2,500) × 4% =	4,700
Opening allowance	4,300
Increase in allowance	400

Journal entry:

		$	
Debit	Irrecoverable debts expense (2,500 + 400)	2,900	
Credit	Receivables		2,500
Credit	Allowance for receivables		400

1   Neville's receivables account shows a balance at the end of the year of $58,200 before making the following adjustments:

   (i)   Newell decides to write off debts amounting to $8,900 as he believes they are irrecoverable.

   (ii)   He also decides to make specific allowance for Carroll's debt of $1,350, Juff's debt of $750 and Mary's debt of $1,416.

   Newell's allowance for receivables at the previous year end was $5,650.

   What is the charge to the statement of profit or loss in respect of the above information?

   A $6,766

   B $11,034

   C $6,829

   D $10,971

2   In the year ended 30 September 20X8, Savannah had sales of $7,000,000. The year-end receivables amounted to 5% of annual sales. At the year end, Savannah's specific allowance for receivables equated to 4% of receivables. She also identified that this amount was 20% higher than at the previous year end. During the year irrecoverable debts amounting to $3,200 were written off and debts amounting to $450 and previously written off were recovered.

   What was the irrecoverable debt expense for the year?

   A $5,083

   B $5,550

   C $5,583

   D $16,750

3   Leo has been notified that a customer has been declared bankrupt. Leo had previously made allowance for this receivable.

   Which of the following is the correct double entry?

A	Debit	Allowance for receivables
	Credit	Receivables
B	Debit	Receivables
	Credit	Irrecoverable debts account
C	Debit	Irrecoverable debts account
	Credit	Receivables
D	Debit	Receivables
	Credit	Allowance for receivables

12 Payables, provisions and contingent liabilities

The following topics are covered in this chapter:

- Cash and credit purchases
- Provisions
- Contingent liabilities and contingent assets

12.1 CASH AND CREDIT PURCHASES

LEARNING SUMMARY

After studying this section you should be able to:

- account for cash and credit purchases
- define a liability

Accounting for cash and credit purchases

If a purchase is for cash, the business pays for the goods/services at the point of sale:

Dr	Purchases / expenses
Cr	Cash

If the purchase is on credit terms the business will pay for the goods/services after receiving them. Typically trading terms allow 30 – 60 days to settle outstanding debts when purchasing goods and services on credit.

KEY POINT Under the accruals concept, the purchase is recorded in the ledger accounts when the expense has been incurred.

When purchasing on credit the expense of the purchase and a corresponding liability needs to be recognised.

DEFINITION   A **liability** is defined as 'a present obligation of the entity arising from past events, the settlement of which is expected to result in an outflow from the entity of resources embodying economic benefits' (IAS 37, para 10).

The accounting entries required for a credit purchase are:

Dr	Purchases / expenses
Cr	Payables

The balance on the payables account is cleared when the payment is made to the credit supplier:

Dr	Payables
Cr	Cash

12.2 PROVISIONS

LEARNING SUMMARY

After studying this section you should be able to:

- understand the definition of 'provision'
- outline the criteria for recognising a provision
- account for a provision.

> **DEFINITION** A **provision** is 'a liability of uncertain timing or amount' (IAS 37, para 10).

KEY POINT Given the uncertainty relating to provisions there is significant scope for accounting error, or even deliberate manipulation when accounting for provisions.

For example, a company may face a legal action for a breach of law. The likely consequence is a fine – it needs to be decided whether this should be reflected in the financial statements.

To reduce the risk of error or manipulation, IAS 37 Provisions, Contingent Liabilities and Contingent Assets states three criteria for recognition of a provision.

Criteria for recognising a provision:
There must be a present obligation (legal or constructive) that exists as the result of past event.
There must be a probable transfer of economic benefits
There must be a reliable estimate of the potential cost.

> **DEFINITION** A **legal obligation** is an obligation that derives from:
>
> - the terms of a contract,
> - legislation, or
> - other operation of law (IAS 37, para 10)

Note the three separate elements of a legal obligation.

> **DEFINITION** A **constructive obligation** is an obligation that derives from an entity's actions where:
>
> - by an established pattern of past practice, published policies, or a sufficiently specific current statement, the entity has indicated to other parties that it will accept certain responsibilities, and
> - as a result, the entity has created a valid expectation on the part of those other parties that it will discharge those responsibilities (IAS 37, para 10)

Note the two separate elements of a constructive obligation.

Accounting for a provision

Upon recognition of a provision there must be an estimate of the potential cost of the uncertain event and immediate recognition in the financial statements. The accounting entries required are:

Dr	Expenses
Cr	Provision

The provision would be classified as a current or non-current liability in the statement of financial position depending on when it is expected the payment will be made.

12.3 CONTINGENT LIABILITIES AND CONTINGENT ASSETS

LEARNING SUMMARY

After studying this section you should be able to:

- understand the definition of 'contingent liability' and 'contingent asset'
- outline the requirements for recognising a contingent liability
- outline the requirements for recognising a contingent asset
- outline the disclosure requirements.

DEFINITION A **contingent liability** is

(a) 'a possible obligation that arises from past events and whose existence will be confirmed only by the occurrence or non-occurrence of one or more uncertain future events not wholly within the control of the entity; or

(b) a present obligation that arises from past events but is not recognised because:

(i) it is not probable that an outflow of resources embodying economic benefits will be required to settle the obligation, or

(ii) the amount of the obligation cannot be measured with sufficient reliability' (IAS 37, para 10).

> An example of a contingent liability is outstanding litigation where the potential costs cannot be estimated with any degree of reliability.

DEFINITION A **contingent asset** is 'a possible asset that arises from past events and whose existence will be confirmed only by the occurrence or non-occurrence of one or more uncertain future events not wholly within the control of the entity' (IAS 37, para 10).

> An example of a contingent asset is a business making a claim for compensation from another party and the outcome of the claim is uncertain at the reporting date.

Accounting for contingent liabilities and contingent assets

Probability of occurrence	Contingent liabilities	Contingent assets
Virtually certain >95%	Provide	Recognise
Probable 51% – 95%	Provide	Disclosure note
Possible 5% – 50%	Disclosure note	Ignore
Remote <5%	Ignore	Ignore

KEY POINT Note that the reporting standard gives no guidance regarding the probabilities of occurrence.

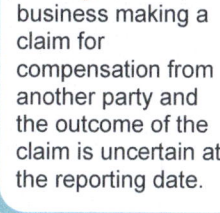

One possible interpretation of the probabilities of occurrence:

Virtually certain > 95%	Probable 51% – 95%
Possible 5% – 50%	Remote < 5%

Provisions should be reviewed at each statement of financial position date and adjusted to reflect the current best estimate.

To increase the provision	
Dr	Expenses
Cr	Provision
To decrease the provision	
Dr	Provision
Cr	Expenses

Disclosure requirements

IAS 37 disclosure requirements:

- When there is a requirement is to provide for a contingent liability, the liability is reflected in the financial statements, but called a provision in order to highlight the uncertainty surrounding it.

- The movement in the provision is recorded in the financial statements each year.

- When disclosure is made by note, the note should state the nature of the contingency, the uncertain factors that may affect the future outcome, and an estimate of the financial effect.

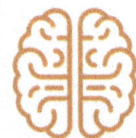

Do you understand?

1   Under what criteria is a provision recognised?

2   The probability of occurrence of a contingent asset is virtually certain and so it can be disclosed within a note to the accounts.

     True or false?

3   Provisions should be reviewed at each statement of financial position date and adjusted to reflect the current best estimate.

     True or false?

1   A provision should be recognised if (a) there is an obligation, (b) a transfer of economic benefits is probable, (c) a reliable estimate can be made.
2   If the probability of occurrence for a contingent asset is virtually certain it would be recognised in the accounts.
3   True.

1   Which of the following items require a provision in accordance with IAS 37 Provisions, Contingent Liabilities and Contingent Assets?

   (i)   An electronics retailer has a policy of providing refunds over and above the statutory requirement to do so. This policy is well publicised and customers have made use of this facility in the past.

   (ii)   A customer has made a legal claim against an entity, claiming that faulty goods sold to them caused injury. The entity's lawyers have advised that the claim will possibly succeed and, if it does, compensation of $5,000 will be payable

   What is the charge to the statement of profit or loss in respect of the above information?

   A   (i) only

   B   (ii) only

   C   (i) and (ii)

   D   Neither

2   **Which of the following statements about the requirements relating to IAS 37 Provisions, Contingent Liabilities and Contingent Assets are correct?**

   (i)   A contingent asset should be disclosed by note if an inflow of economic benefits is probable.

   (ii)   No disclosure of a contingent liability is required if the possibility of a transfer of economic benefits arising is remote.

   (iii) Contingent assets must not be recognised in financial statements unless an inflow of economic benefits is virtually certain to arise.

   A   All three statements are correct.

   B   (i) and (ii) only

   C   (i) and (iii) only

   D   (ii) and (iii) only

3   Recently, users of a new anti-aging serum have suffered blistering of the skin along with considerable pain and discomfort. Following investigation by the manufacturer, Magical Beauty Buys, it appears that product contamination occurred during the bottling process which was performed by Jasmine Co. Magical Beauty Buys legal representatives have advised it that it is probable that customers will make valid compensation claims totalling $2 million and that it is probable Magical Beauty Buys will be able to successfully counter-claim against Jasmine Co for the same amount.

How should this information be reported in the financial statements of Magical Beauty Buys for the year ended 30 June 20X9?

A   There should be a provision for $2 million only recognised in the statement of financial position.

B   There should be a provision and an asset, each for $2 million, recognised in the statement of financial position.

C   No provision or asset should be recognised in the statement of financial position as the two amounts cancel each other.

D   There should be a provision for $2 million in the statement of financial position and a disclosure note only to deal with the contingent asset of the amount which may be recovered from Jasmine Co.

13 **Capital structure and finance costs**

The following topics are covered in this chapter:

- Sources of finance
- Accounting for share issues
- Dividends
- Loan notes and preferences shares
- Other reserves
- Income tax

13.1 SOURCES OF FINANCE

LEARNING SUMMARY

After studying this section you should be able to:

- understand the capital structure of a limited liability company.

Debt and equity

Finance is provided by capital investment in the company, either in the form of debt (loan) capital or equity (share) capital.

| Debt | ┄┄➤ | The holder of debt is entitled to some form of mandatory repayment e.g. interest, repayment of capital. |

| Equity | ┄┄➤ | An equity holder is not entitled to any repayment. Instead they share the 'residual assets' of the business when it ceases to trade. |

KEY POINT Most forms of finance are simple to categorise but some forms of finance have characteristics of both and it's not entirely clear whether they are debt, equity or both.

Financial capital

Three forms of financial capital	
Ordinary 'equity' share capital	This is equity as the directors have no obligation to pay a dividend. Ordinary shares are classified within equity in the statement of financial position.
Loan notes	Loan notes are a form of debt and are classified as a liability in the statement of financial positon. The directors are required to pay the loan holder an annual interest amount with the full debt repaid at a later date in time. The interest payments are treated as a finance charge which is shown as an expense in the statement of profit or loss.
Preference shares	Preference shares can either be debt or equity depending on their contractual terms.

Preference shares

```
                    ┌─────────────────┐
            ┌───────▶│   Redeemable    │┄┄┄▶
            ┊        └─────────────────┘
┌───────────────┐
│   Types of    │
│  preference   │
│    shares     │
└───────────────┘
            ┊        ┌─────────────────┐
            └───────▶│  Irredeemable   │┄┄┄▶
                     └─────────────────┘
```

- Obligation to repay is evidence of debt.
- Classified as a liability in the statement of financial position.
- Dividends shown as finance charges in the statement of profit or loss.

- No obligation to repay is evidence of equity.
- Classified as equity.
- Dividends treated the same way as ordinary dividends.

DEFINITION A **dividend** is an amount paid to the shareholders as a return for investing in the company.

13.2 ACCOUNTING FOR SHARE ISSUES

LEARNING SUMMARY

After studying this section you should be able to:

- understand the different forms of share issues and be able to account for them.

DEFINITION The **nominal value** is the price of the share when it was issued, rather than its current market value.

Issuing at market price	
The company must always receive at least the nominal value per share. The amount in excess of nominal value issued is classified as share premium.	
Debit	Bank account (issue price x no. of shares)
Credit	Share capital account (nominal value × no. of shares)
Credit	Share premium account (premium raised × no. of shares)

Rights issue	
An offer by the company to issue shares to current shareholders in proportion to their existing shareholding. It is normally made at less than market value in order to encourage shareholders to take up the share issue.	
Debit	Bank account (issue price x no. of shares)
Credit	Share capital account (nominal value × no. of shares)
Credit	Share premium account (premium raised × no. of shares)

Bonus issue	
A 'free' issue of shares to current shareholders in proportion to their existing shareholding i.e. no cash or any other consideration received in exchange for the share issue. It is a way for the company to capitalise its reserves and increase the number of shares in issue, which also reduces the market value per share.	
Debit	Share premium/retained earnings (nominal value x no. of shares)
Credit	Share capital account (nominal value x no. of shares)

A bonus issue may also be referred to as a capitalisation issue.

13.3 DIVIDENDS

LEARNING SUMMARY

After studying this section you should be able to:

- account for the payment of a dividend.

Many listed companies may pay dividends in two instalments. The first instalment is paid during the financial year and is known as an interim dividend. The second instalment is usually paid after the end of the financial year and is known as a final dividend.

The total of the dividends paid in a financial year is included in the statement of changes in equity as a reduction in retained earnings.

KEY POINT It is important to understand that dividends paid by a company are not an expense included in the statement of profit or loss.

Dividends are an appropriation of profit by the company to its shareholders.

The accounting entries to record a dividend are:

Dr	Retained earnings
Cr	Bank

KEY POINT Dividends are accounted for in the financial statements on a 'cash paid' basis.

13.4 LOAN NOTES AND PREFERENCE SHARES

LEARNING SUMMARY

After studying this section you should be able to:

- define and account for a loan note
- understand why a preference share is considered to be a form of debt finance and how it is classified within the financial statements.

Loan notes

DEFINITION A **loan note** is a fixed term loan.

KEY POINT The term 'loan note' refers to the document that is evidence of the debt, often a certificate that is issued to the lender.

Loan notes have a set nominal value, like a share. Loan notes are sold at an agreed price – the price does not have to be the same as the nominal value. The life of the loan note will be fixed and the company issuing them will have to pay the loan note holder back at an agreed point in time.

The issuer will have to pay interest to the loan note holder. The interest will be calculated based on the nominal value of the loan note. The interest incurred is included in finance costs in the statement of profit or loss.

To record the issue of the loan note:

Dr	Cash
Cr	Non-current liability

To record the finance charge recognised each year:

Dr	Finance charges
Cr	Cash /current liabilities

> The credit entry to cash or current liabilities depends on whether the interest is paid out in the year or not.

13.5 OTHER RESERVES

LEARNING SUMMARY

After studying this section you should be able to:

- identify and record the other reserves which may appear in the company statement of financial position

Companies can also use the capital created internally to generate wealth by reinvesting it back into the business:

Revaluation reserve ·········▸ Records unrealised gains on the revaluation of property, plant and equipment.

This reserve cannot be used to pay out a dividend.

Retained earnings ·········▸ Records the total of net profits and losses to date that have been retained within the business.

Retained earnings can be used to pay out a dividend.

13.6 INCOME TAX

LEARNING SUMMARY

After studying this section you should be able to:

- record income tax in the statement of profit or loss of a company, including the under and overprovision of tax in the prior year.

The income generated by a business entity is also subject to tax:

- **Sole traders and partnerships** – the tax charge is imposed on the individual, not the business.

- **Limited liability companies** – as a separate legal entity, if it generated income it is subject to tax:

  It is normally referred to as 'income tax':

  - **Statement of profit or loss** – a tax charge is recognised as an expense.

  - **Statement of financial position** – must reflect any tax liabilities outstanding

KEY POINT Company year-ends and tax year-ends rarely match. Therefore companies must estimate their income tax liability at the end of each accounting period and record an appropriate estimate of the liability likely to be paid.

Steps to recording income tax

Step 1	
At the end of the year a company should make the following double entry for its estimate of the tax liability:	
Debit	Income tax charges (P&L)
Credit	Income tax liability (SoFP – current liability)
Step 2	
Following the year-end the actual tax liability will be calculated and paid. The associated double entry is:	
Debit	Income tax liability
Credit	Cash
Step 3	
It is unlikely the actual charge will match the estimated liability so the tax liability account will be left with a closing balance carried forward.	
If there is an overprovision in the prior year (i.e. estimate was greater than the amount paid) there will be a closing credit balance carried forward. This is adjusted as follows:	
Debit	Income tax liability
Credit	Income tax charge
If there is an underestimate in the prior year (i.e. estimate was less than the amount paid) there will be a closing debit balance carried forward. This is adjusted as follows:	
Debit	Income tax charge
Credit	Income tax liability

Tax in the financial statements

	$
Tax charge estimated for the year (liability in the statement of financial position)	X
Less: overprovision in earlier year	(X)
OR:	
Add: under-provision in earlier year	X
Tax charge (expense in the statement of profit or loss)	X

Do you understand?

1   Dividends paid are an expense to be recognised in the statement of profit or loss.

True or false?

2   How is a bonus issue of shares accounted for?

3   What is the nominal value of a share?

4   If there is an underestimate in the prior year of the income tax charge how is the closing debit balance within the income tax liability account adjusted for?

1   False. Dividends are an appropriation of profit by the company to its shareholders.
2   Debit share premium/retained earnings Credit share capital (by the nominal value x no of shares).
3   The nominal value is the price of the share when it was issued, rather than its current market value.
4   Debit income tax charge Credit income tax liability.

1   **Which TWO of the following statements are true?**

    A   Redeemable preference shares are classified as a liability on the statement of financial position.

    B   Irredeemable preference shares are classified as a liability on the statement of financial position.

    C   Redeemable preference shares are classified as equity on the statement of financial position.

    D   Irredeemable preference shares are classified as equity on the statement of financial position.

2   An entity, Spark, makes an issue of 20,000 $1 equity shares at a price of $1.75.

    What accounting entries are required to account for the transaction?

Debit or credit	Ledger account	$

3   An entity, Taylor, has issued equity share capital of 250,000 shares with a nominal value of $0.50 each and a share premium account balance of $100,000.

    What accounting entries are required if Taylor was to make a bonus issue of one share for four held?

	Debit		*Credit*	
A	Share capital	$62,500	Share premium	$62,500
B	Share premium	$31,250	Share capital	$31,250
C	Share capital	$31,250	Share premium	$31,250
D	Share capital	$62,500	Share premium	$62,500

4   Astral Co has a debit balance relating to income tax of $500 included in its trial balance extracted on 30 June 20X4. Astral estimated that its income tax liability for the year ended 30 June 20X4 was $8,000.

    What amounts should be included in Astral Co's financial statements for the year ended 30 June 20X4?

	Statement of profit or loss	*Statement of financial position*
A	$8,000	$8,000
B	$8,500	$8,000
C	$7,500	$8,500
D	$8,000	$7,500

14 Accounting reconciliations

The following topics are covered in this chapter:
- Bank reconciliations
- Control account reconciliations
- Petty cash reconciliations

14.1 BANK RECONCILIATIONS

LEARNING SUMMARY

After studying this section you should be able to:
- understand the purpose of a bank reconciliation
- perform a bank reconciliation.

The purpose of a bank reconciliation

The objective of a bank reconciliation is to reconcile the cash book and bank statement balances.

KEY POINT It checks the accuracy of an organisation's bank account record by comparing it with the record of the account held by the bank.

The cash book is the double entry record of cash and bank balances contained within the general ledger. It may be referred to as the cash control account.

The contents of the cash book should be exactly the same as the record provided by the bank in the form of a bank statement, and therefore the business' records should correspond with the bank statement. However there are discrepancies that may occur:

> Debits and credits are reversed in bank statements because the bank is recording the transaction from its own point of view.

Unrecorded items – these are items which arise in the bank statements before they are recorded in the cash book.

Examples of unrecorded items:
- interest
- bank charges
- dishonoured cheques.

As unrecorded items are not known by the business until they see the bank statement, the cash book must be adjusted to reflect these items.

Timing differences – these items have been recorded in the cash book, but due to the bank clearing process have not yet been recorded in the bank statement:

- Outstanding/unpresented cheques (cheques sent to suppliers but not yet cleared by the bank).

- Outstanding/uncleared lodgements (cheques received by the business but not yet cleared by the bank).

The bank statement balance must be adjusted for these items on the bank reconciliation statement.

If the business has made a mistake in the cash book, the cash book balance will need to be adjusted to correct it.

If the bank has made a mistake, e.g. record a transaction relating to a different person within our business' bank statement, the bank statement balance will need to be adjusted for these items.

Proforma bank reconciliation

Cash book				
	$			$
Bal b/fwd	X	Bal b/fwd		X
Adjustments	X	Adjustments		X
Revised bal c/fwd	X	Revised bal c/fwd		X
	—			—
	X			X
	—			—
Revised bal b/fwd	X	Revised bal b/fwd		X

Adjustments are made for unrecorded items and errors in the cash book.

Bank reconciliation statement as at …..	
Balance per bank statement	**X**
Add: outstanding cheques	X
Less: outstanding lodgements	(X)
Add / less: other adjustments to the bank statement	X/(X)
Balance per cash book (revised)	**X**

If the bank reconciliation proforma starts with 'Balance per cash book' we have to reverse the adjustments to reconcile back to the 'Balance per bank statement'.

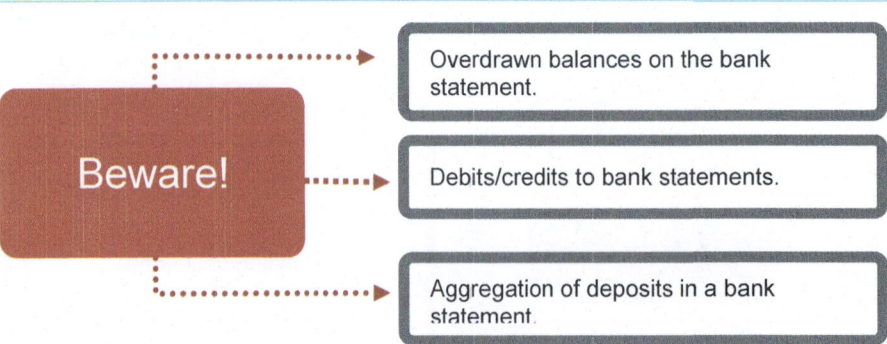

Beware!

Overdrawn balances on the bank statement.

Debits/credits to bank statements.

Aggregation of deposits in a bank statement.

KEY POINT The bank balance on the statement of financial position is always the balance per the revised cash book.

Steps to perform a bank reconciliation

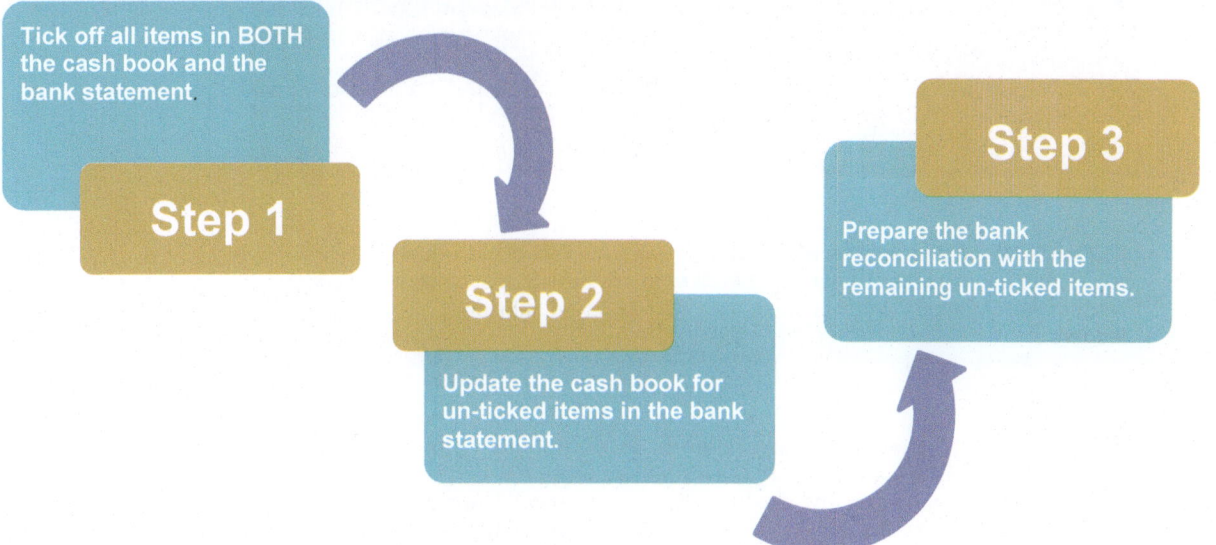

Step 1
Tick off all items in BOTH the cash book and the bank statement.

Step 2
Update the cash book for un-ticked items in the bank statement.

Step 3
Prepare the bank reconciliation with the remaining un-ticked items.

14.2 CONTROL ACCOUNT RECONCILIATIONS

LEARNING SUMMARY

After studying this section you should be able to:

- understand the purpose of control accounts
- account for contras between receivables and payables
- prepare control account reconciliations
- understand the purpose of a supplier statement.

DEFINITION **Control accounts** are general (nominal) ledger accounts that summarise a large number of transactions.

Control accounts are used to prove the accuracy of the ledger accounting system.

Control accounts are mainly used with regard to receivables and payables:

| Receivables | = | Trade receivables ledger control |
| Payables | = | Trade payables ledger control account |

Postings to the control accounts from day books

From the sales day book to the trade receivables ledger control account:	
Dr	Trade receivables ledger control account
Cr	Sales revenue

Most entities will also maintain 'memorandum accounts' as well as control accounts.

From the purchases day book to the trade payables ledger control account:	
Dr	Purchases
Cr	Trade payables ledger control account

> **DEFINITION** **Memorandum accounts** are separate lists of individual receivable and payable amounts due from or to customers or suppliers respectively. Memorandum accounts may also be called subsidiary ledgers.

KEY POINT Introducing the use of control accounts might appear as though entries are duplicated. Individual accounts for receivables and payables and separate control accounts cannot both form part of the double-entry system. Either one or the other of these must be treated as being outside the double-entry system.

The receivables ledger control account may include any of the following entries:

Receivables ledger control account			
Balance b/d	X	Balance b/d	X
Credit sales (SDB)	X	Cash from customers (CB)	X
Dishonoured cheques (CB)	X	Sales returns (SRDB)	X
Refunds of credit balances (CB)	X	Irrecoverable debts	X
Interest charged	X	Discounts allowed	X
Balance c/d	X	Contra with PLCA	X
		Balance c/d	X
	X		X

SDB = sales day book

SRDB = sales returns day book

CB = cash book

The payables ledger control account may include any of the following entries:

Payables ledger control account			
Balance b/d	X	Balance b/d	X
Cash paid to suppliers (CB)	X	Credit purchases (PDB)	X
Contra with RLCA	X	Refunds of debit balances (CB)	X
Discounts received	X	Balance c/d	X
Purchases returns (PRDB)	X		
Balance c/d	X		
	X		X

Any entries to the control accounts must also be reflected in the individual accounts within the accounts receivable and payable ledgers.

PDB = purchases day book

PRDB = purchases returns day book

CB = cash book

KEY POINT A control account reconciliation is a working to ensure that the entries in the ledger accounts (memorandum) agree with the entries in the control account. The totals in each should be exactly the same.

Contra entries

The situation may arise where a customer is also a supplier. Instead of both owing each other money, it may be agreed that the balances are contra'd, i.e. cancelled.

Dr	Payables ledger control account
Cr	Receivables ledger control account

The memorandum accounts must also be updated.

Steps to prepare a control account reconciliation

To ensure that the postings have been recorded correctly in both the general and subsidiary ledger, you need to reconcile them on a regular basis.

1	Balance the control account in the general ledger
2	Balance the individual accounts in the subsidiary ledger
3	List the subsidiary account names and balances
4	Compare the balance on the control account to the total of the subsidiary accounts

Due to the nature of the exam, you will not be asked to produce a full control account reconciliation. Instead you may be asked for the revised balance on the control account/list of individual balances after one or two errors have been corrected.

The examiner will provide details of the error(s). You must decide for each whether correction is required in the control account, the list of individual balances or both. When all errors have been corrected, the revised balance on the control account should agree to the revised total of the list of individual balances.

Supplier statements

DEFINITION **Supplier statements** are issued to a business by suppliers to summarise the transactions that have taken place during a given period, and also to show the balance outstanding at the end of the period.

The purpose of a supplier statement is to ensure that the amount outstanding is accurate and agrees with underlying documentation.

KEY POINT The payables (individual) ledger account should agree with the total of the supplier statement. It is a further way to prove the accuracy of accounting records.

14.3 PETTY CASH RECONCILIATIONS

LEARNING SUMMARY

After studying this section you should be able to:

- perform a petty cash reconciliation.

Steps to perform a petty cash reconciliation

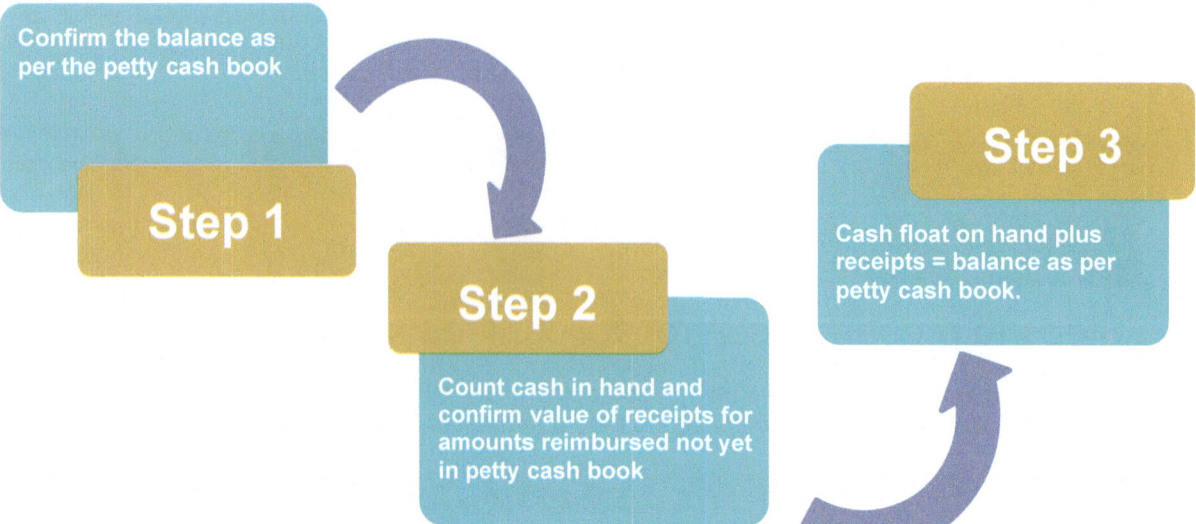

Confirm the balance as per the petty cash book

Step 1

Step 2

Count cash in hand and confirm value of receipts for amounts reimbursed not yet in petty cash book

Step 3

Cash float on hand plus receipts = balance as per petty cash book.

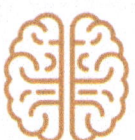

Do you understand?

1   Discounts received appear on what side of the purchases ledger control account?

2   Which statement is correct?

(i)   An uncleared lodgement has been recorded in the cash book but not on the bank statement

(ii)   An uncleared lodgement is shown on the bank statement but not in the cash book

(iii)   Uncleared lodgements are not reconciling items.

3   Dishonoured cheques appear on the credit side of the receivables ledger control account.

True or false?

---

1   Discounts received appear on the debit side of the purchases ledger control account as discounts received reduce the liability.

2   Statement (i) is correct as uncleared lodgements are cheques received by the business and so recorded in the cash book but not yet cleared by the bank.

3   False. Dishonoured cheques will require the receivable to be reinstated as payment has not been received, therefore an entry is made to the debit side of the receivables ledger control account.

1   The cash book of Worcester shows a credit balance of $1,350.
     Cheques of $56 have been written to suppliers but not yet cleared the
     bank; uncleared lodgements amount to $128. The bank has
     accidentally credited Worcester's account with interest of $15 due to
     another customer. A standing order of $300 has not been accounted
     for in the general ledger.

     What is the balance on the bank statement?

     A $993 Cr

     B $993 Dr

     C $1,707 Cr

     D $1,707 Dr

2   **Which of the following statements about bank reconciliations are
     correct?**

     (1)   In preparing a bank reconciliation, unpresented cheques must
           be deducted from a balance of cash at bank shown in the bank
           statement.

     (2)   A cheque from a customer paid into the bank but dishonoured
           must be corrected by making a debit entry in the cash book.

     (3)   An error by the bank must be corrected by an entry in the cash
           book.

     (4)   An overdraft is a debit balance in the bank statement.

     A   (1) and (3)

     B   (2) and (3)

     C   (1) and (4)

     D   (2) and (4)

3   Your firm's cash book at 30 April 20X8 showed a balance at the bank
     of $2,490. Comparison with the bank statement at the same date
     revealed the following differences:

	$
Unpresented cheques	840
Bank charges not in cash book	50
Receipts not yet credited by the bank	470
Dishonoured cheque not in cash book	140

     The correct bank balance at 30 April 20X8 was:

     A $1,460

     B $2,300

     C $2,580

     D $3,140

4   A payables ledger control account showed a credit balance of
     $768,420. The payables ledger totalled $781,200.

     **Which one of the following possible errors could account in full
     for the difference?**

     A   A contra against a receivables ledger debit balance of $6,390
          has been entered on the credit side of the payables ledger
          control account.

     B   Cash purchases cash purchases of $28,400 was entered to the
          debit side of the payables ledger control account instead of the
          correct figure for discounts received of $15,620.

     C $12,780 cash paid to a supplier was entered on the credit side
          of the supplier's account on the payables ledger.

     D   The total of discounts received $6,390 has been entered on the
          credit side of the payables ledger control account.

5   A receivables ledger control account showed a debit balance of
     $37,642. The individual customers' accounts in the receivables ledger
     showed a total of $35,840.

     The difference could be due to:

     A   Undercasting the sales day book by $1,802

     B   Overcasting the sales returns day book by $1,802

     C   Entering cash receipts of $1,802 on the debit side of a
          customer's account

     D   Entering a contra with the payables ledger control account of
          $901 on the debit side of the receivables ledger control account

15 The trial balance, errors and suspense accounts

The following topics are covered in this chapter:

- The trial balance
- Types of errors
- Suspense accounts
- Adjustments to profit

15.1 THE TRIAL BALANCE

LEARNING SUMMARY

After studying this section you should be able to:

- identify the purpose of and prepare the trial balance.

DEFINITION The **trial balance** is a list showing the balance brought down on each ledger account in the general ledger. It is a check point to ensure that every debit has an equal and opposite credit entry.

> The totals of the trial balance columns should balance. However it does not confirm that the account you have debited/credited is correct.

Proforma trial balance

	Debit $	Credit $
Revenue		X
Purchases	X	
Administrative expenses	X	
Non-current assets	X	
Trade receivables	X	
Cash	X	
Share capital		X
Loans		X
Trade payables		X
	X	X

15.2 TYPES OF ERRORS

LEARNING SUMMARY

After studying this section you should be able to:

- identify different types of errors that can occur in an accounting system
- correct errors where the trial balance still balances.

Types of errors

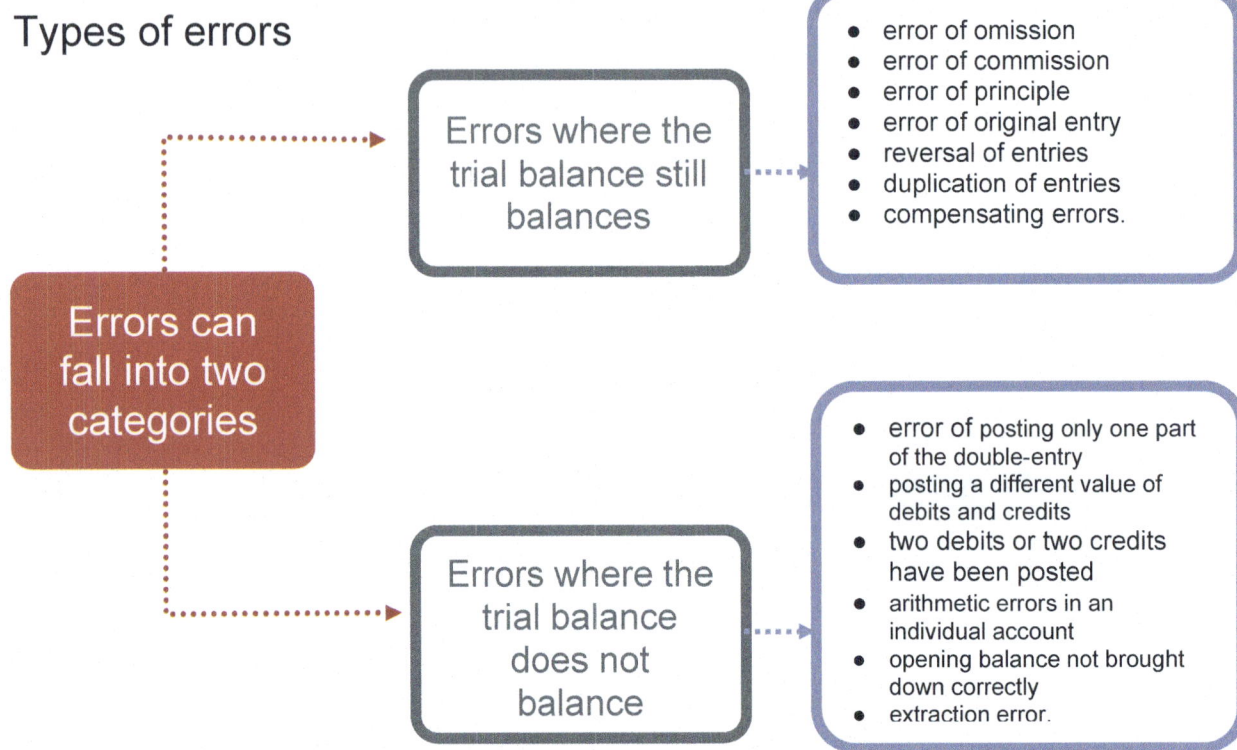

Errors can fall into two categories

Errors where the trial balance still balances

- error of omission
- error of commission
- error of principle
- error of original entry
- reversal of entries
- duplication of entries
- compensating errors.

Errors where the trial balance does not balance

- error of posting only one part of the double-entry
- posting a different value of debits and credits
- two debits or two credits have been posted
- arithmetic errors in an individual account
- opening balance not brought down correctly
- extraction error.

DEFINITIONS An **error of omission** is where a transaction has been completely omitted from the accounting records.

An **error of commission** is where a transaction has been recorded in the wrong account, but it is the correct nature i.e. an expense being posted to the wrong type of expense account.

An **error of principle** is where a transaction has conceptually been recorded incorrectly i.e. an expense has been capitalised.

An **error of original entry** is where the correct double entry has been made but with the wrong amount.

Reversal of entries is where the correct amount has been posted to the correct accounts but on the wrong side.

A **compensating error** is where two different errors have been made which cancel each other out.

KEY POINT The trial balance provides a useful control mechanism for detecting errors; however a balanced trial balance does not guarantee the accuracy of the financial statements.

Errors where the trial balance still balances

When correcting these errors, a good approach is to consider:

Step 1: What should the double entry have been?

Step 2: What was the double entry?

Step 3: What correction is required?

Always assume that if one side of the double entry is not mentioned, it has been recorded correctly.

Errors where the trial balance does not balance

If there is a difference on the trial balance, then a suspense account is used to make the total debits equal the total credits

The balance on the suspense account must be cleared before final accounts can be prepared.

15.3 SUSPENSE ACCOUNTS

LEARNING SUMMARY

After studying this section you should be able to:

- understand the purpose of a suspense account

- correct errors where the trial balance does not balance.

DEFINITION A **suspense account** is an account in which debits or credits are held temporarily until sufficient information is available for them to be posted to the correct accounts.

Suspense accounts are used for two purposes:

- On the extraction of a trial balance the debits are not equal to the credits and the difference is put to a suspense account.

- When a bookkeeper performing double entry is not sure where to post one side of an entry they may debit or credit a suspense account and leave the entry there until its ultimate destination is clarified.

KEY POINT Correction to any errors where the trial balance does not balance will affect the suspense account.

When correcting these errors the approach to take is very similar to the steps seen before with the exception of:

- In step 2 use the suspense account to balance off the entry that was made (remember: the double entry must have been unbalanced for the TB not to balance).

- In step 3 for the correcting journal, reverse this suspense account entry.

Refer back to the steps required for errors where the trial balance still balances.

15.4 ADJUSTMENTS TO PROFIT

After studying this section you should be able to:

* understand how adjustments impact profit.

The correction journal may result in a change in profit, depending on whether the journal debits or credits the statement of profit or loss:

Dr Statement of financial position account Cr Statement of financial position account	No impact on profit
Dr Profit or loss account Cr Profit or loss account	No impact on profit
Dr Profit or loss account Cr Statement of financial position account	Profit decreases
Dr Statement of financial position account Cr Profit or loss account	Profit increases

KEY POINT For this purpose the suspense account is defined as a statement of financial position account.

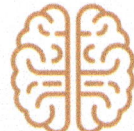

Do you understand?

1 An accounting entry to pay rent expense of $500 via the bank was entered into Leo's accounts as:

Dr rent $500 Cr bank $5,000.

What type of error is this an example of?

2 If an accounting entry is debited to the statement of profit or loss and credited to the statement of financial position what impact does it have on profit?

   (i)   No impact on profit

   (ii)   Profit increases

   (iii)   Profit decreases

3 A compensating error is where the correct amount has been posted to the correct accounts but on the wrong side.

True or false?

1 This is an example of an error of original entry.
2 (iii) profit decreases.
3 False. This is the description for the reversal of entries. A compensating error is where two different errors have been made which cancel each other out.

1 **Which of the following are limitations of the trial balance?**

    (1)   It does not include final figures to be included in the financial statements.

    (2)   It does not identify errors of commission.

    (3)   It does not identify in which accounts errors have been made.

    A   (1) and (2)

    B   (2) and (3) only

    C   All of the above

    D   None of the above

2 **Which TWO of the following errors could cause the total of the debit column and the total of the credit column of the trial balance not to agree?**

    A   A casting error of $300 made when totalling the sales day book.

    B   A transposition error made when posting the total of cash payments into the general ledger.

    C   Discount received was included in the trial balance as a debit balance.

    D   A cheque paid to a supplier recorded was debited to cash and correctly recognised in trade payables.

3 A trial balance shows a total of debits of $347,800 and a total of credits of $362,350.

    (1)   A credit sale of $3,670 was incorrectly entered in the sales day book as $3,760.

    (2)   A non-current asset with a carrying amount of $7,890 was disposed of for $9,000. The only accounting entry was to debit cash.

    (3)   The allowance for receivables was increased from $8,900 to $10,200. The allowance account was debited in error.

After adjusting for the errors above, what is the balance on the suspense account?

    A $26,150 debit

    B $26,060 debit

    C $26,240 debit

    D $2,950 credit

16 Preparing basic financial statements

The following topics are covered in this chapter:

- Preparing financial statements – the process
- The presentation of the financial statements
- The financial statements
- Events after the reporting period

16.1 PREPARING FINANCIAL STATEMENTS – THE PROCESS

LEARNING SUMMARY

After studying this section you should be able to:

- outline the process to prepare financial statements.

Balance off and close the ledger accounts

Prepare a trial balance

Year-end adjustments made and ledgers closed off

Trial balance used to prepare financial statements

> At this stage you should be familiar with the double entry bookkeeping process, closing off the ledger accounts and extracting a trial balance.

> Examination questions may draw on any particular stage of this process.

> The financial statements are reviewed in detail later.

16.2 ADJUSTMENTS TO THE INTIAL TRIAL BALANCE

LEARNING SUMMARY

After studying this section you should be able to:

- identify the common adjustments made to at the end of the period.

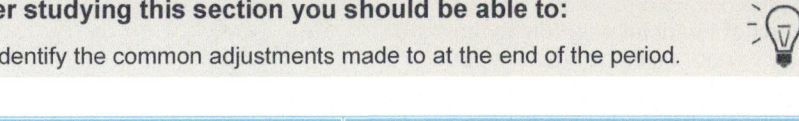

Closing inventory	Depreciation charge
Accruals and prepayments	Irrecoverable debts and allowances for receivables
Income tax	Provisions and contingent liabilities
Events after the reporting period	Correction of errors

16.3 PRESENTATION OF THE FINANCIAL STATEMENTS

The following components must be presented:

- **A statement of financial position**

- **A statement of profit or loss**

- **A statement of other comprehensive income**

- **A statement of changes in equity**

- **Notes to the accounts**

- **A statement of cash flows**.

16.4 THE FINANCIAL STATEMENTS

The statement of financial position

Statement of financial position for *(name of business)* as at *(date of period end)*		
	$	$
Non-current assets		
Property, plant and equipment	X	
Investments	X	
Intangibles	X	
		X
Current assets		
Inventories	X	
Trade and other receivables	X	
Prepayments	X	
Cash	X	
		X
Total assets		X
Equity		
Ordinary share capital	X	
Irredeemable preference share capital	X	
Share premium	X	
Reserves:		
Retained earnings	X	
		X
Non-current liabilities		
Loan notes		X
Current liabilities		
Trade and other payables	X	
Overdrafts	X	
Tax payable	X	
		X
Total equity and liabilities		X

The statement of profit or loss

Statement of profit or loss for *(name of business)* for the period ended *(date of period end)*		
		$
Revenue		X
Cost of sales		(X)
Gross profit		**X**
Distribution costs		(X)
Administrative expenses		(X)
Profit from operations		**X**
Investment income		X
Finance costs		(X)
Profit before tax		**X**
Tax expense		(X)
Net profit for the period		**X**

Relationship between the statement of profit or loss and the statement of financial position

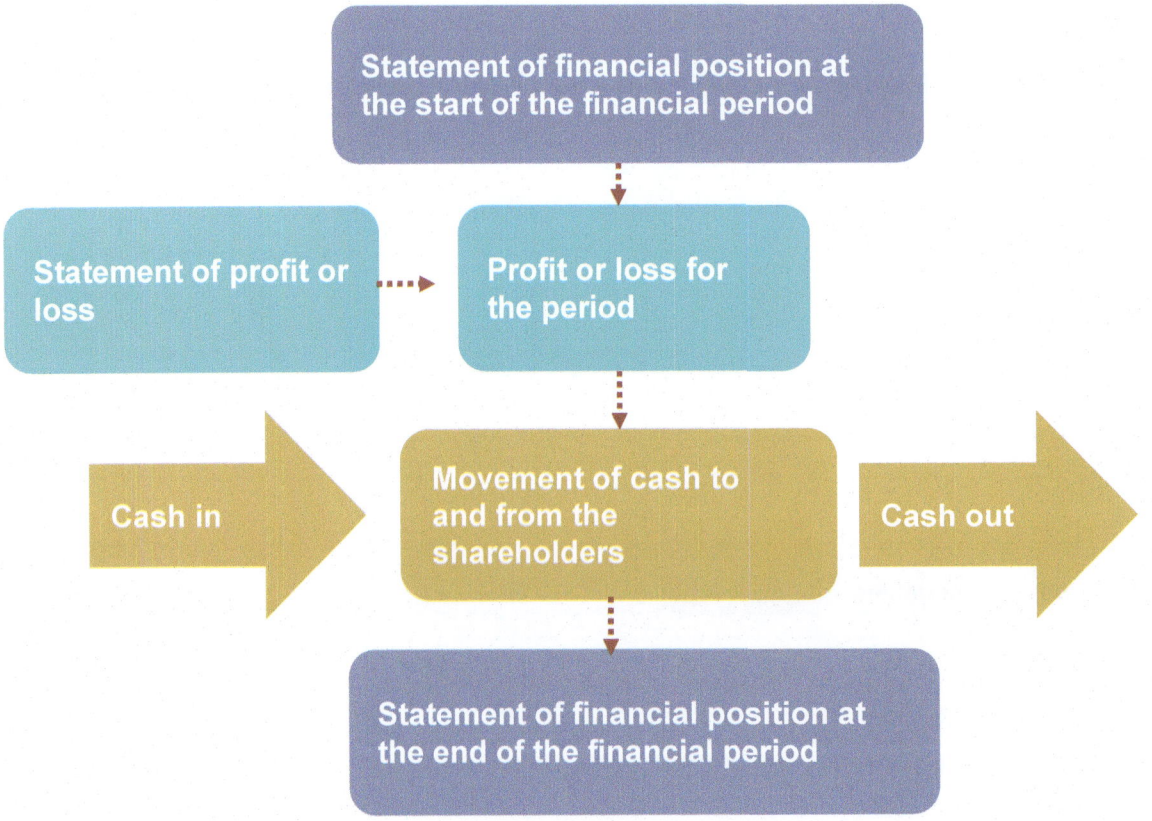

The statement of comprehensive income

Statement of profit or loss for *(name of business)* for the period ended *(date of period end)*	
	$
Revenue	X
Cost of sales	(X)
Gross profit	**X**
Distribution costs	(X)
Administrative expenses	(X)
Profit from operations	**X**
Investment income	X
Finance costs	(X)
Profit before tax	**X**
Tax expense	(X)
Net profit for the period	**X**
Other comprehensive income	
Items that will not be reclassified to profit or loss in future periods:	
Gain/loss on property revaluation in the year	X/(X)
Total comprehensive income for the year	**X**

KEY POINT An entity can choose to present the above information in the form of two separate statements:

• the statement of profit or loss for the year, and

• the statement of other comprehensive income for the year.

The statement of changes in equity

	Share capital	Share premium	Revaluation surplus	Retained earnings	Total
	$	$	$	$	$
Balance at the beginning of the financial period	X	X	X	X	X
Equity shares issued	X	X			X
Revaluation surplus in the year			X		X
Net profit				X	X
Dividends				(X)	(X)
Balance at the end of the financial period	X	X	X	X	X

Disclosure notes

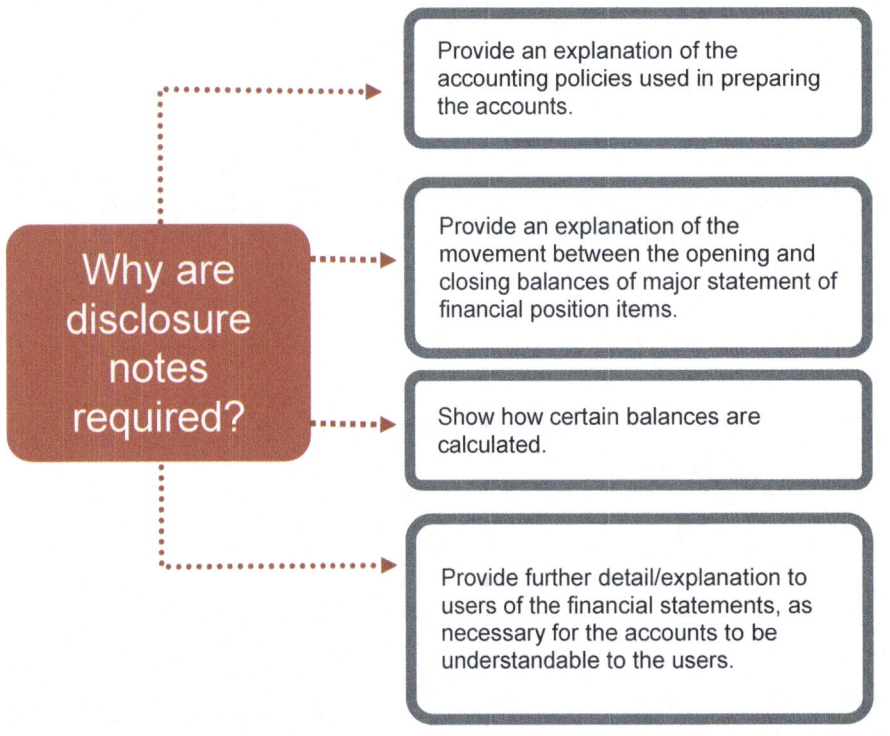

Why are disclosure notes required?

Provide an explanation of the accounting policies used in preparing the accounts.

Provide an explanation of the movement between the opening and closing balances of major statement of financial position items.

Show how certain balances are calculated.

Provide further detail/explanation to users of the financial statements, as necessary for the accounts to be understandable to the users.

The examination requires understanding of the notes for:
• non-current and intangible assets
• provisions
• events after the reporting date
• inventory.

16.5 EVENTS AFTER THE REPORTING PERIOD

LEARNING SUMMARY

After studying this section you should be able to:

- understand the accounting of events after the reporting period.

DEFINITION **Events after the reporting period** are 'those events, favourable and unfavourable, that occur between the end of the reporting period and the date when the financial statements are authorised for issue' (IAS 10, Para 3).

KEY POINT The purpose of IAS 10 is to define to what extent events that occur after the reporting period should be recognised in the financial statements.

Adjusting events - material events which provide additional evidence of conditions already in existence at the reporting date.

··· ▶ The financial statements should be adjusted to include the effect of such events.

Non-adjusting events - material events which do not concern conditions existing at the reporting date.

··· ▶ Impact going concern. ··· ▶ Adjust financial statements to present on the break-up basis.

··· ▶ Does not impact going concern. ··· ▶ Do not adjust the financial statements but disclose as a note if important to users' understanding.

Examples of adjusting events:
Discovery of errors or fraud that occurred during the reporting period
Resolution of an insurance claim or court case that confirms an obligation at the reporting date
Major customers going into liquidation

Examples of non-adjusting events
Fluctuations in tax/exchange rates
Issue of shares
Fire or flood after the reporting date

16.6 REVENUE FROM CONTRACTS WITH CUSTOMERS

LEARNING SUMMARY

After studying this section you should be able to:

* understand the accounting of revenue from contracts with customers.

> **DEFINITION** **Revenue** is 'income arising in the course of an entity's ordinary activities' (IFRS 15, Appendix A).

IFRS 15 Revenue from contracts with customers specifies a five-step approach to recognition of revenue:

Step 1
Identify the contract with the customer

Step 2
Identify the performance obligations in the contract

Step 3
Determine the transaction price

Step 4
Allocate the transaction price to the performance obligations in the contract

Step 5
Recognise revenue when (or as) the entity satisfies a performance obligation

> **KEY POINT** The purpose of IAS 10 is to define to what extent events that occur after the reporting period should be recognised in the financial statements.

Note that, when applying the five-step approach, revenue will be recognised on one of two bases:

* **over a period of time** - likely to apply for the provision of services when there is simultaneous provision and consumption of a service, or

* **at a point in time** – likely to apply for the sales of goods when transfer of control can be determined at a specific point in time.

Do you understand?

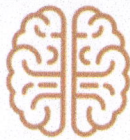

1   Give two examples of non-adjusting events.

2   The statement of financial position summarises the asset, liability and equity balances (i.e. the financial position of the entity) at the end of the accounting period.

    True or false?

3   Dividends paid will be deducted from what balance on the statement of changes in equity?

    (i)   share capital

    (ii)   share premium

    (iii)   revaluation surplus

    (iv)   retained earnings

4   On what two bases can revenue be recognised?

---

1   Examples of non-adjusting events are; fluctuations in tax/exchange rates, the issue of shares and fire or flood occurring after the reporting date.

2   True.

3   (iv) dividends paid are deducted from the retained earnings balance.

4   Revenue can be recognised on one of two bases.

- **over a period of time** - likely to apply for the provision of services when there is simultaneous provision and consumption of a service, or
- **at a point in time** – likely to apply for the sales of goods when transfer of control can be determined at a specific point in time.

Exam style questions

1   The following information relates to Minnie's hairdressing business in the year ended 31 August 20X7:

	$
Expenses	7,100
Opening inventory	1,500
Closing inventory	900
Purchases	12,950
Gross profit	12,125
Inventory drawings of shampoo	75

What is the sales figure for the business?

A $32,700

B $25,600

C $25,675

D $25,750

2   The following information is relevant to Wimbledon:

	$
Opening inventory	12,500
Closing inventory	17,900
Purchases	199,000
Distribution costs	35,600
Administrative expenses	78,800
Audit fee	15,200
Carriage in	3,500
Carriage out	7,700
Depreciation	40,000

Depreciation is to be split in the ratio 70:30 between the factory and the office. All office expenses are classified as administrative expenses.

Based upon the available information, what was Wimbledon's cost of sales?

A $233,600

B $221,600

C $225,100

D $237,100

3   **Where, in a set of financial statements complied in accordance with international accounting standards, would you expect to find dividends paid?**

(1)   Statement of profit or loss and other comprehensive income.

(2)   Statement of financial position.

(3)   Statement of cash flows.

(4)   Statement of changes in equity.

A   (1) and (3)

B   (2) and (3)

C   (1) and (4)

D   (3) and (4)

4   You have been asked to help prepare the financial statements of Willow for the year ended 30 June 20X1. The entity's trial balance as at 30 June 20X1 is shown below.

	Debit	Credit
	$000	$000
Share capital		50,000
Share premium		25,000
Revaluation reserve at 1 July 20X0		10,000
Land & buildings – value/cost	120,000	
accumulated depreciation at 1 July 20X0		22,500
Plant and equipment – cost	32,000	
accumulated depreciation at 1 July 20X0		18,000
Trade and other receivables	20,280	
Trade and other payables		8,725
5% bank loan repayable 20X5		20,000
Cash and cash equivalents	2,213	
Retained earnings at 1 July 20X0		12,920
Sales		100,926
Purchases	67,231	
Distribution costs	8,326	
Administrative expenses	7,741	
Inventories at 1 July 20X0	7,280	
Dividends paid	3,000	

The following information is relevant to the preparation of the financial statements:

(i)   The inventories at the close of business on 30 June 20X1 cost $9,420,000.

(ii)   Depreciation is to be provided for the year to 30 June 20X1 as follows:

Buildings 4% per annum Straight line basis

This should all be charged to administrative expenses

Plant and equipment 20% per annum Reducing balance basis

This is to be apportioned as follows:

	%
Cost of sales	70
Distribution costs	20
Administrative expenses	10

Land, which is non-depreciable, is included in the trial balance at a value of $40,000,000. At 30 June 20X1, a surveyor valued it at $54,000,000. This revaluation is to be included in the financial statements for the year ended 30 June 20X1.

(iii) It has been decided to write off a debt of $540,000 which will be charged to administrative expenses.

(iv)   Included within distribution costs is $2,120,000 relating to an advertising campaign that will commence on 1 January 20X1 and run to 31 December 20X1.

(v)   Loan interest has not yet been accounted for.

(vi)   The tax charge for the year has been calculated at $2,700,000.

Required:

Prepare the statement of profit or loss and other comprehensive income of Willow for the year ended 30 June 20X1 and the statement of financial position as at 30 June 20X1.

17 Incomplete records

- Incomplete records
- The accounting equation approach
- The ledger account approach
- Cash and bank summaries approach
- Profit ratios – mark-up and margin approach

17.1 INCOMPLETE RECORDS

LEARNING SUMMARY

After studying this section you should be able to:

- identify the different approaches to finding incomplete information.

When you are preparing a set of accounts, you may not have all of the information available to you to complete a set of financial statements. Missing figures have to be calculated from the best information available. you will have to use the best information that is available to you to calculate any missing figures.

The different approaches that may be used are:

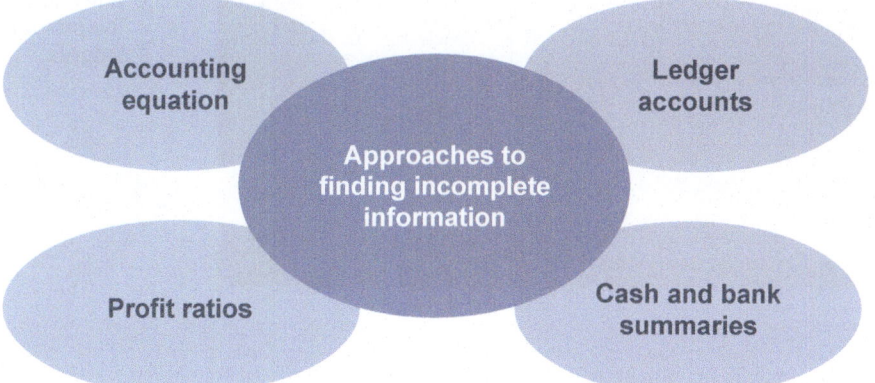

17.2 THE ACCOUNTING EQUATION APPROACH

LEARNING SUMMARY

After studying this section you should be able to:

- use the accounting equation to calculate missing information.

The accounting equation is:

Assets = **Liabilities** + **Equity**

A scenario may require the accounting equation to be rearranged or data may be provided as a listing of accounts for assets, liabilities and equity – refer to the different expansions.

The accounting equation may also be expanded:

Total assets = share capital + retained earnings + other reserves + total liabilities

Retained earnings (RE) may be further broken down into:

Closing RE = the prior year's RE figure +/– this year's profit/loss – dividends

17.3 THE LEDGER ACCOUNT APPROACH

LEARNING SUMMARY

After studying this section you should be able to:
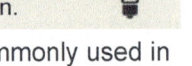

- use the ledger account approach to calculate missing information.

The balancing figure approach, using ledger accounts, is commonly used in the following way:

Receivables	Credit sales, Money received from receivables
Payables	Credit purchases, Money paid to payables
Expenses	Charge for the year
Cash at bank	Drawings, Money stolen
Cash in hand	Cash sales, Cash stolen

The transactions referred to here are those which are commonly asked as 'incomplete data'. However a scenario may ask to calculate any entry as seen in the proforma ledgers.

Refer to cash and bank summaries approach

Receivables ledger control account proforma

Receivables ledger control account			
Balance b/d	X	Cash from customers	X
Sales	X	Sales returns	X
		Irrecoverable debts	X
		Discounts allowed	X
		Contra with PLCA	X
		Balance c/d	X
	X		X

The ledger accounts provided in this chapter are not exhaustive – information may be provided to reconstruct any type of ledger account to work out incomplete information.

Payables ledger control account proforma

Payables ledger control account			
Cash paid to suppliers	X	Balance b/d	X
Contra with RLCA	X	Purchases	X
Discounts received	X		
Purchases returns	X		
Balance c/d	X		
	X		X

Expense account proforma

Expenses account			
Prepayment b/d	X	Accrual b/d	X
Bank	X	Charge to the SPL	X
Accrual c/d	X	Prepayment c/d	X
	X		X

Prepayment b/d is an opening prepayment.
Accrual b/d is an opening accrual.
Prepayment c/d is a closing prepayment.
Accrual b/d is a closing accrual.

17.4 CASH AND BANK SUMMARIES APPROACH

LEARNING SUMMARY

After studying this section you should be able to:

- use cash and bank summaries to calculate missing information.

Cash and bank figures can be calculated using the ledger account approach or by reconstructing cash inflows and outflows using the bank statement.

Cash at bank account proforma

Cash at bank account			
Balance b/d	X	Cash paid to suppliers	X
Cash received from customers	X	Expenses	X
Bankings from cash in hand	X	Drawings	X
Sundry income	X	Balance c/d	X
	X		X

The opening and closing balances on the cash at bank account could be on either the debit or credit side depending on whether the balance is in funds or overdrawn.

Cash in hand account proforma

Cash in hand account			
Balance b/d	X	Cash purchases	X
Cash sales	X	Cash expenses	X
Sundry other receipts	X	Cash banked	X
		Cash drawings	X
		Balance c/d	X
	X		X

17.5 PROFIT RATIOS – MARK-UP AND MARGINS APPROACH

LEARNING SUMMARY

After studying this section you should be able to:

- use profit ratios to calculate missing information.

Gross profit can be expressed as a percentage of either sales or cost of sales:

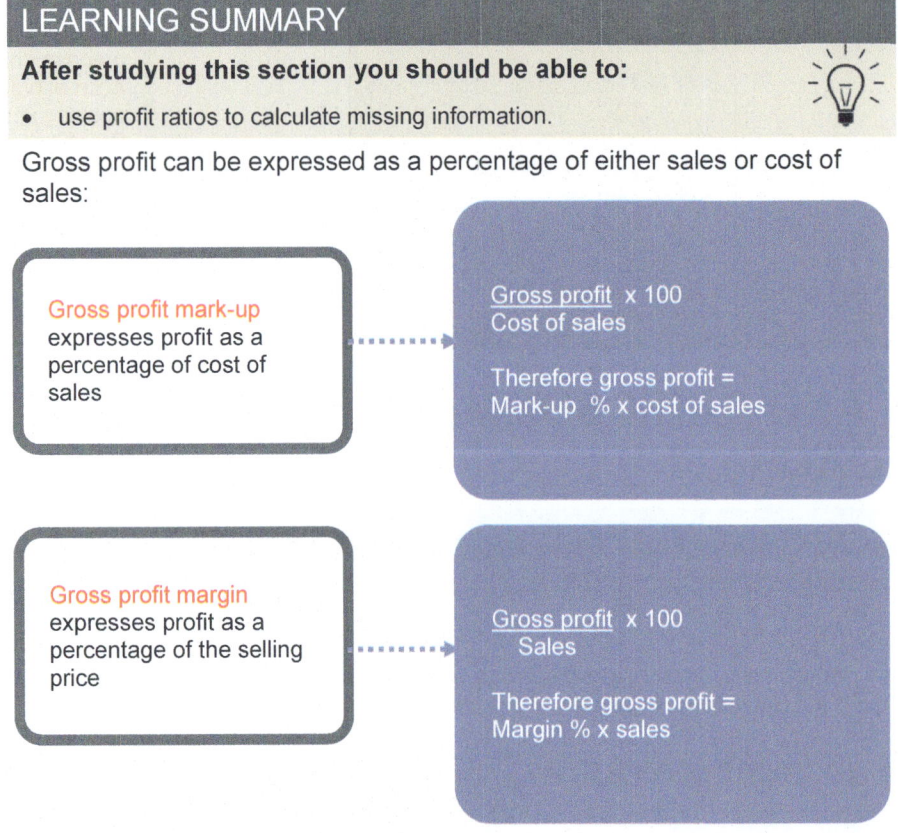

Gross profit mark-up expresses profit as a percentage of cost of sales

$$\frac{\text{Gross profit}}{\text{Cost of sales}} \times 100$$

Therefore gross profit = Mark-up % x cost of sales

Gross profit margin expresses profit as a percentage of the selling price

$$\frac{\text{Gross profit}}{\text{Sales}} \times 100$$

Therefore gross profit = Margin % x sales

Cost structures relationships:

	Gross profit mark-up	Gross profit margin
Sales	100% + mark-up %	100%
Cost of sales	100%	100% - margin %
Gross profit	Mark-up %	Margin %

Exam questions will often provide information about gross profit figures and ratios. A missing figure can be calculated using the 'relationship' columns.

118

Do you understand?

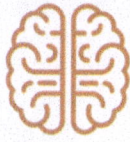

1   Name the four approaches that can be taken to calculate incomplete information.

2   What side of the receivables ledger control account do the following entries appear on?

    (i)   Discounts allowed

    (ii)   Credit sales

    (iii)   Contra with payables ledger control account

3   Cash at hand is banked. What is the accounting entry to reflect this?

4   What does a gross profit mark-up express and how is it calculated?

5   What does a gross profit margin express and how is it calculated?

1   P is a sole proprietor whose accounting records are incomplete. All the sales are cash sales and during the year $50,000 was banked, including $5,000 from the sale of a business car. He paid $12,000 wages in cash from the till and withdrew $2,000 per month as drawings. The cash in the till at the beginning and end of the year was $300 and $400 respectively.

What was the value of P's sales for the year?

A $80,900

B $81,000

C $81,100

D $86,100

2   You have been provided with the following incomplete and incorrect extract from the statement of profit or loss of a business that trades at a mark-up of 25% on cost:

	$	$
Sales		174,258
Less: Cost of goods sold:		
Opening inventory	12,274	
Purchases	136,527	
Closing inventory	X	
	_____	
		(X)
		_____
Gross profit		X
		_____

Having discovered that the sales revenue figure should have been $174,825 and that purchase returns of $1,084 and sales returns of $1,146 have been omitted, what should be the amount for closing inventory?

A $8,662

B $8,774

C $17,349

D $17,458

3 A fire in the offices of Lewis has destroyed most of the accounting records. The following information has been retrieved:

	$
Sales	630,000
Opening inventory	24,300
Closing inventory	32,750
Opening payables	29,780
Closing payables	34,600

Gross profit for the period should represent a mark-up of 40%.

What was the total cash paid to suppliers in the year?

A $8,662

B $8,774

C $17,349

D $17,458

4 Pike runs an angling shop in the south of Spain. He spends all of his spare time fishing and consequently has kept no accounting records in the year ended 31 August 20X5. He knows that he has taken $6,800 cash out of his business during the year plus bait which cost the business $250. He can also remember putting his $20,000 winnings on the Spanish lottery into the business in March.

Pike knows that at the last year end his business had assets of $40,000 and liabilities of $14,600. He has also calculated that the assets of the business at 31 August 20X5 are worth $56,000, and the liabilities $18,750.

What profit or loss has Pike made in the year?

A $1,100 profit

B $1,100 loss

C $1,350 profit

D $1,350 loss

18 Statement of cash flows

The following topics are covered in this chapter:

- The purpose and format of a statement of cash flows
- Cash flows from operating activities
- Cash flows from investing activities
- Cash flows from financing activities

18.1 THE PURPOSE AND FORMAT OF A STATEMENT OF CASH FLOWS

LEARNING SUMMARY

After studying this section you should be able to:

- differentiate between profit and cash flow
- understand the purpose of preparing a statement of cash flows
- outline the format of a statement of cash flows.

Profit and cash

Whilst a business entity might be profitable this does not mean it will be able to survive. To survive a business needs cash to be able to pay its debts. If it cannot pay its debts, the business would become insolvent and could not continue to operate.

KEY POINT Profit is not the same as cash flow.

Why does profit not equal the change in cash and bank balances?

Profit is calculated on an accruals basis. Bank and cash balances change when monies are received and paid out.

The accruals basis means income and expense are recognised when earned or incurred not when cash is received or paid.

The calculation of profit includes some items that do not affect cash at all or affect it differently.

Examples:
- Depreciation is deducted from profit but involves no movement in cash.
- The profit or loss on disposal of a non-current asset is included in profit for the year, but it is the proceeds of sale that affect the cash and bank balances.
- Any change in the allowance for receivables will affect profit for the year, but will not affect cash flows.

Bank and cash balances are affected by some items that do not affect profit.

Examples:
- Purchase of non-current assets (only depreciation affects profit)
- Raising additional capital
- Repayment of loans.

IAS 7 Statement of cash flows requires companies to prepare a statement of cash flows as part of their annual financial statements. The statement of cash flows must be presented using standard headings.

The format of a statement of cash flows

Statement of cash flows	
	$
Cash flows from operating activities	
Cash generated from operations	X
Interest paid	(X)
Taxation paid	(X)
Net cash from operating activities	X
Cash flows from investing activities	
Purchase of non-current assets	(X)
Proceeds from the sale of non-current assets	X
Interest received	X
Dividends received	X
Net cash from investing activities	X
Cash flows from financing activities	
Issue of shares	X
Loan repaid	(X)
Loan issued	X
Dividends paid	(X)
Net cash from financing activities	X
Net increase/ (decrease) in cash and cash equivalents	X(/X)
Cash and cash equivalents b/fwd	X
Cash and cash equivalents c/fwd	X

Change in cash balances from principal revenue producing activities.

Change in cash balances from gains or losses from investments.

Change in cash balances from activities raising and repaying finance.

18.2 CASHFLOWS FROM OPERATING ACTIVITIES

LEARNING SUMMARY

After studying this section you should be able to:

- calculate the cash flow from operating activities using the indirect and direct method

- calculate the figures needed for the statement of cash flows including cash flows from operating activities.

There are two methods of presenting cash flows from operations:

- **Direct method** – based upon cash flow information extracted directly from the accounting records. This method discloses information that would otherwise remain confidential and so most business entities do not use the direct method.

> You need to learn both methods of presentation and be able to apply either method in the examination if required.

Cash flows from operating activities	
	$
Cash receipts from customers	X
Cash payments to suppliers	(X)
Cash payments to employees	(X)
Cash payments for expenses	(X)
Cash generated from operations	X
Interest paid	(X)
Tax paid	(X)
Net cash flow from operations	(X)/X

- **Indirect method** – relies upon information that is disclosed in or calculated from the financial statements. The starting point is normally profit before tax, which is adjusted to remove any non-cash items or accruals-based figures included in the statement of profit or loss.

Depreciation	Added back to profit before tax as it is a non-cash expense.
Profit or loss on disposal of non-current assets	Non-cash income or expense so deducted or added back – cash proceeds on disposal are classified as an investing activity.
Investment income and finance costs	Finance costs are added back and investment income is deducted as they are not part of cash generated from operations.
Movement in inventory	Inventory represents purchases made in one period, which will be charged against profit in another period. An increase in inventory is deducted from profit before tax as it is a cash outflow to pay for additional inventory. A decrease in inventory is added to profit before tax as it is a cash inflow from disposing of inventory
Movement in receivables	Receivables represent revenue recognised in one period, with the cash being received in next. A decrease in receivables is added to profit before tax (cash inflow) as more cash has been collected from receivables. An increase in trade receivables is deducted from profit before tax.
Movement in payables	Payables represent purchases made in one period, which will be paid in the next. An increase means the business has had the use or benefit of the entity but not paid for them - cash reserves are preserved. A decrease in payables means more payables have been paid - deducted from profit before tax as a cash outflow.

. Cash flows from operating activities	
	$
Profit before taxation	X
Depreciation/amortisation charge	X
(Profit)/loss on disposal of non-current assets	(X)/X
Investment income	(X)
Finance costs	X
Operating profit before working capital changes	X
(Increase)/decrease in inventories	(X)/X
(Increase)/decrease in trade and other receivables	(X)/X
Increase/(decrease) in trade and other payables	X/(X)
Cash generated from operations	X
Interest paid	(X)
Tax paid	(X)
Net cash flow from operating activities	X/(X)

Cash flows may also include:

- interest paid
- tax paid

A ledger account approach or a list approach can be used to help with calculations.

KEY POINT The cash flow should be calculated by reference to the charge to profits for the item (shown in the statement of profit or loss) and any opening or closing payable balance (shown on the statement of financial position).

Interest / tax payable			
	$		$
		Bal b/fwd (SFP)	X
Cash paid (β)	X	Expense for the year (SPL)	X
Bal c/fwd (SFP)	X		
	—		—
	X		X
	—		—

18.3 CASHFLOWS FROM INVESTING ACTIVITIES

LEARNING SUMMARY

After studying this section you should be able to:

- calculate the figures needed for the statement of cash flows including cash flows from investing activities.

Investing activities cash inflows may include:

- interest received

- dividends received

- proceeds of sale of non-current assets.

Investing activities cash outflows may include:

- purchase of property, plant and equipment.

Interest and dividends received

The calculation of interest received and dividends received should take account of both the income shown in the statement of profit or loss and any relevant receivables balance from the opening and closing statements of financial position.

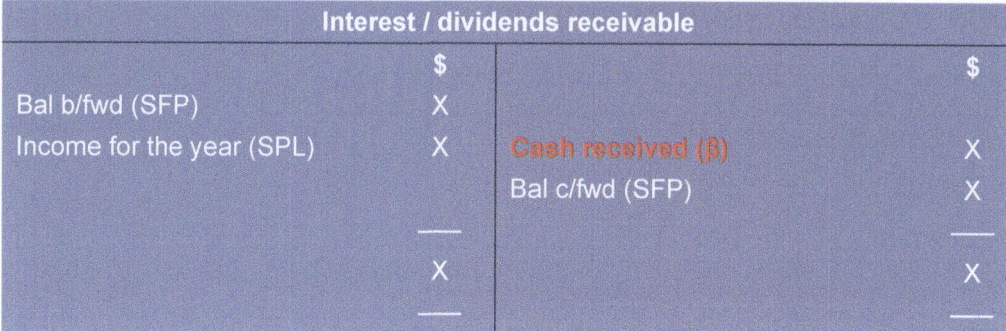

Interest / dividends receivable			
	$		$
Bal b/fwd (SFP)	X		
Income for the year (SPL)	X	Cash received (β)	X
		Bal c/fwd (SFP)	X
	___		___
	X		X
	___		___

Proceeds from the sale of non-current assets

Proceeds from the sale of non-current assets can be calculated if the carrying amount of the non-current asset being disposed is known and whether a profit or loss has been made on disposal.

- If a profit has been made on disposal, the proceeds can be calculated by adding the profit to the carrying amount of the disposed asset.

- If a loss has been made on disposal, the proceeds can be calculated by deducting the loss from the carrying amount of the disposed asset.

Purchase of property, plant and equipment

The purchase of property, plant and equipment and resulting cash outflow can be calculated with a ledger account approach.

NCA – carrying amount			
	$		$
Bal b/fwd (SFP)	X	Disposals at carrying amount	X
Additions (cash paid) (β)	X	Depreciation charge	X
Revaluation	X	Bal c/fwd (SFP)	X
	___		___
	X		X
	___		___

18.4 CASHFLOWS FROM FINANCING ACTIVITIES

LEARNING SUMMARY

After studying this section you should be able to:

- calculate the figures needed for the statement of cash flows including cash flows from financing activities.

Financing activities cash inflows may include:

- proceeds of the issue of shares

- proceeds of receipt of loans/debentures.

Financing activities cash outflows may include:

- repayment of loans/debentures

- dividends paid

- interest paid.

> **KEY POINT** IAS 7 permits interest paid to be classified as a cash outflow within either operating activities or as a financing activity.

> Ensure that the cash outflow for interest paid in the year is classified either within operating activities or within financing activities and not included twice within the statement of cash flows.

Proceeds from the issue of shares

Proceeds from the issue of shares can be calculated by comparing the amounts included in the statement of financial position brought forward and carried forward on two accounts:

- share capital

- share premium.

> **KEY POINT** If there is a bonus issue made in the year; this will not result in a cash inflow.

Proceeds of receipt of loans or repayment of loans

The cash flows in relation to a loan can be calculated by comparing the amounts included in the statement of financial position brought forward and carried forward.

A fall in the amount outstanding indicates that all or part of the loan has been repaid in the year (a cash outflow). An increase indicates that there has been a further loan received in the year (a cash inflow).

Dividends paid

As dividends paid are effectively paid out of retained earnings, it is usually necessary to reconcile the opening and closing balances on retained earnings to identify any dividend paid in the year as a balancing figure.

> **KEY POINT** IAS 7 permits dividends paid to be classified as either an operating cash flow or as a financing cash flow. It is more usual to classify dividends paid as a financing cash flow.

Do you understand?

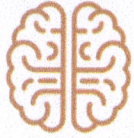

1   If a profit has been made on disposal, the proceeds can be calculated by deducting the profit from the carrying amount of the disposed asset.

   True or false?

2   IAS 7 Statement of cash flows requires companies to prepare a statement of cash flows as part of their annual financial statements. Activities are split into three categories – what are those categories?

3   Name a cash inflow from a financing activity.

4   Explain both the direct and indirect method to present cash flows from operating activities.

1   State whether each of the following statements is true or false.

A   A statement of cash flows prepared using the direct method produces a different figure for investing activities in comparison with that produced if the indirect method is used.

B   A bonus issue of shares does not feature in a statement of cash flows.

C   The amortisation charge for the year on intangible assets will appear as an item under 'Cash flows from operating activities' in a statement of cash flows.

D   Loss on the sale of a non-current asset will appear as an item under 'Cash flows from investing activities' in a statement of cash flows.

2   Extracts from the financial statements of Deuce Co showed balances as follows:

	20X9	20X8
$1 Share capital	300,000	120,000
Share premium	260,000	100,000

A bonus issue of 1 share for every 12 held at the 20X8 year-end occurred during the year and loan notes of $300,000 were issued at par. Interest of $12,000 was paid during the year.

What is the net cash inflow from financing activities?

A $480,000

B $605,000

C $617,000

D $640,000

3   A business has made a profit of $8,000 but its bank balance has fallen by $5,000.

Which one of the following statements could be a possible explanation for this situation?

A   Depreciation charge of $3,000 and an increase in inventories of $10,000

B   Depreciation charge of $6,000 and the repayment of a loan of $7,000

C   Depreciation charge of $12,000 and the purchase of new non-current assets for $25,000

D   The disposal of a non-current asset for $13,000 less than its carrying amount

4 A statement of cash flows prepared in accordance with the indirect method reconciles profit before tax to cash generated from operations.

Which of the following lists of items consists only of items that would be ADDED to profit before tax?

A   Decrease in inventory, depreciation charge, profit on sale of non-current assets

B   Increase in payables, decrease in receivables, profit on sale of non-current assets

C   Loss on sale of non-current assets, depreciation charge, increase in receivables

D   Decrease in receivables, increase in payables, loss on sale of non-current assets

5 The following financial statements and supporting information relate to Firework, a limited liability entity:

Statement of profit or loss and other comprehensive income for the year ended 30 June 20X5

	$000
Revenue	113,250
Cost of sales	(77,500)
Gross profit	35,750
Distribution costs	(3,000)
Administration expenses	(1,000)
Interest payable	(750)
Profit before tax	31,000
Income tax expense	(6,000)
Profit for the year	25,000
Other comprehensive income:	
Revaluation of property, plant and equipment	2,000
Total comprehensive income for the year	27,000

Statement of financial position at 30 June 20X5

	20X5 $000	20X4 $000
ASSETS		
Non-current assets		
Property, plant and equipment	110,000	93,000
Current assets		
Inventories	36,000	30,000
Trade receivables	40,000	35,000
Cash and equivalents	Nil	10,000
Total assets	186,000	168,000

EQUITY AND LIABILITIES

Equity share capital	20,000	15,000
Share premium	8,000	3,000
Revaluation reserve	10,000	8,000
Retained earnings	96,000	85,000
	_____	_____
Total equity	134,000	111,000
Non-current liabilities		
Bank loan	7,000	17,000
Current liabilities		
Trade payables	36,500	30,000
Income tax	6,500	10,000
Bank overdraft	2,000	Nil
	_____	_____
Total equity and liabilities	186,000	168,000
	_____	_____

Notes:

The following information is relevant to the financial statements of Firework:

(i)   During the year ended 30 June 20X5, Firework disposed of several items of plant and equipment for sale proceeds of $8,000,000. The loss on disposal of $2,000,000 is included within cost of sales. The depreciation charge for the year was $15,000,000.

(ii)   Firework estimated that the income tax liability arising on the profit for the year ended 30 June 20X5 was $6,500,000.

Required:

Based upon the available information, prepare a statement of cash flows using the indirect method for Firework for the year ended 30 June 20X5 in accordance with the requirements of IAS 7 *Statement of Cash Flows*.

19 Interpretation of financial statements

The following topics are covered in this chapter:
- Interpreting financial information
- Ratio analysis
- Profitability ratios
- Liquidity and efficiency ratios
- Financial position ratios

19.1 INTERPRETING FINANCIAL INFORMATION

LEARNING SUMMARY

After studying this section you should be able to:

- understand what interpretation of financial information aims to achieve.

It is important that users of financial statements can interpret the financial statements to be able to draw out valid conclusions. Ratio analysis is widely used for this purpose.

Interpretation involves comparisons of:

- prior years
- forecasts
- competitor performance.

Users can compare sales and expense figures, asset and liability balances and cash flows to perform this analysis.

KEY POINT Ratio analysis is a tool to assist understanding and comparison.

> Note that ratio analysis is about both understanding financial data and what it means as well as enabling comparisons.

19.2 RATIO ANALYSIS

LEARNING SUMMARY

After studying this section you should be able to:

- outline what ratio analysis is and the classification of ratios.

Calculating and interpreting ratios provides users with further insight into the following areas:

| Profitability | Liquidity and efficiency | Financial position |

KEY POINT Ratios use simple calculations based upon the interactions within sets of data.

When analysing financial data and using ratios to do so, consider the following questions:

- What does the ratio mean?
- What does a change in the ratio mean?
- What is the norm or expectation for this particular industry?
- What are the limitations of the ratio?

> Scenarios may ask for a calculation or demonstration of understanding of the ratios and performance area.

19.3 PROFITABILITY RATIOS

LEARNING SUMMARY

After studying this section you should be able to:

- calculate and understand the meaning of profitability ratios.

Profitability ratios:
- Gross profit margin
- Net profit margin
- Return on capital employed
- Net asset turnover

Gross profit margin

> **DEFINITION**   On a unit basis the **gross profit** represents the difference between the unit sales price and the direct cost per unit.

The margin works this out on an average basis across all sales for the year.

The gross profit margin % is calculated as follows:

$$\frac{\text{Gross profit}}{\text{Sales revenue}} \times 100$$

Changes may be due to:
- selling prices
- product mix
- purchase costs
- production costs
- inventory valuations.

Operating profit margin

> **DEFINITION**   The **operating profit margin** is an expansion of the gross profit margin. It includes all of the items that come after gross profit but before finance charges and taxation, such as distribution and administration costs in the statement of profit or loss.

The operating profit margin % is calculated as follows:

$$\frac{\text{Operating profit}}{\text{Sales revenue}} \times 100$$

If the gross profit margin has remained static but the operating profit margin has changed, consider the following possible causes:
- changes in employment patterns (recruitment, redundancy etc.)
- changes to depreciation due to large acquisitions or disposals
- significant write-offs of irrecoverable debt
- changes in rental agreements
- significant investments in advertising
- rapidly changing fuel costs.

Return on capital employed (ROCE)

DEFINITION ROCE measures how much operating profit is generated for every $1 capital invested in the business.

The return on capital employed % is calculated as follows:

$$\frac{\text{Operating profit}}{\text{Capital employed}} \times 100$$

KEY POINT Capital employed can be measured in either of the two following ways:

• equity plus interest-bearing finance, i.e. non-current loans plus share capital and reserves or

• total assets less current liabilities.

Either method will provide the same end answer to calculate capital employed.

Net asset turnover

DEFINITION The **net asset turnover** measures management's efficiency in generating revenue from the net assets at its disposal.

The net asset turnover is similar to ROCE but instead we measure the amount of sales revenue generated for every $1 capital invested in the business.

The net asset turnover (number of times per annum) is calculated as

$$\frac{\text{Sales revenue}}{\text{Capital employed (net assets)}}$$

Relationship between ratios

ROCE can be subdivided into operating profit margin and asset turnover:

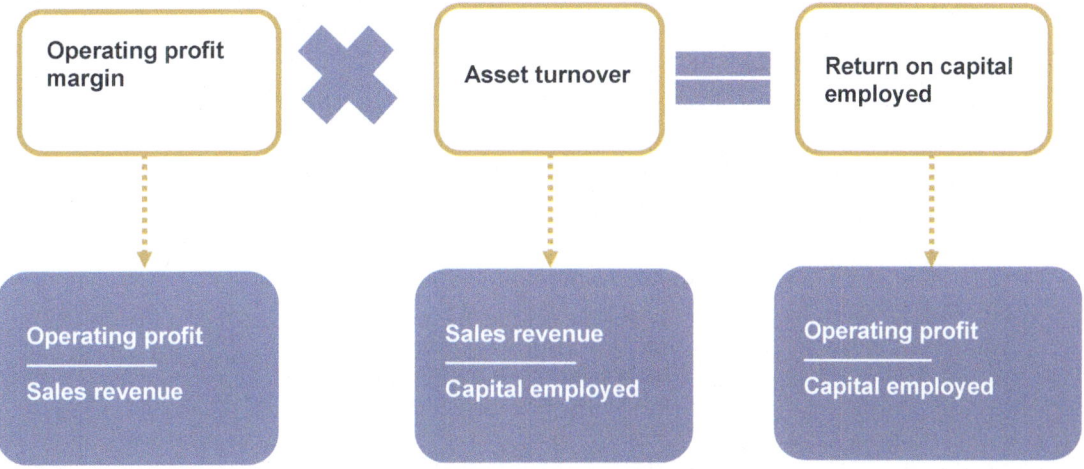

19.4 LIQUIDITY AND EFFICIENCY RATIOS

LEARNING SUMMARY

After studying this section you should be able to:

- calculate and understand the meaning of liquidity and efficiency ratios.

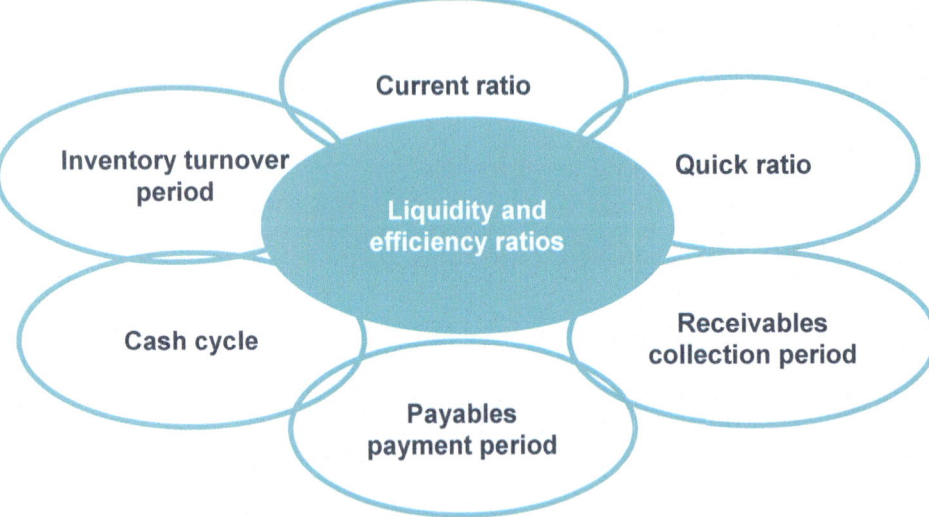

Current ratio

> **DEFINITION** The **current ratio** measures the adequacy of current assets to meet liabilities as they fall due.

The current ratio is calculated as follows:

$$\frac{\text{Current assets}}{\text{Current liabilities}} : 1$$

An increasingly high current ratio may appear safe but may be due to:
- high levels of inventory and receivables – indicating inventory that cannot be sold and poor credit control over receivables.
- high cash levels – indicating a loss of investment opportunities.

KEY POINT Traditionally, a current ratio of 2:1 or higher was regarded as appropriate for most businesses to maintain creditworthiness. However, more recently a figure of 1.5:1 is regarded as the norm.

Consideration must be given to the nature of the business. For example supermarkets tend to have few trade receivables, high levels of trade payables and tight cash control to fund investment

Quick ratio (acid test)

> **DEFINITION** The **quick ratio** is also known as the acid test ratio because by eliminating inventory from current assets it provides the acid test of whether the company has sufficient liquid resources (receivables and cash) to settle its liabilities.

The quick ratio is calculated as follows:

$$\frac{(\text{Current assets} - \text{inventory})}{\text{Current liabilities}} : 1$$

When interpreting the quick ratio, care should be taken over the status of the bank overdraft. A business with a low quick ratio may have no issue paying amounts due if sufficient overall overdraft facilities are available.

Inventory turnover period

The inventory turnover period is calculated as follows:

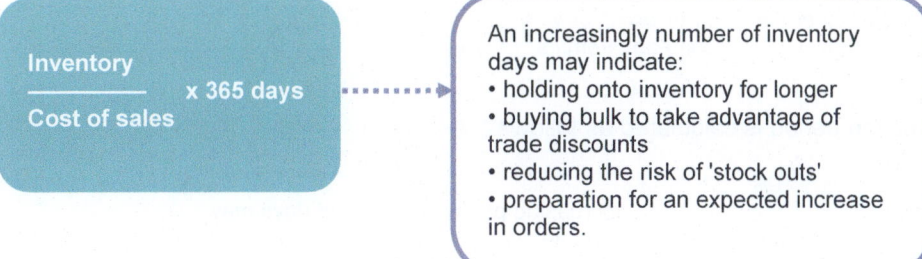

$$\frac{\text{Inventory}}{\text{Cost of sales}} \times 365 \text{ days}$$

An increasingly number of inventory days may indicate:
- holding onto inventory for longer
- buying bulk to take advantage of trade discounts
- reducing the risk of 'stock outs'
- preparation for an expected increase in orders.

Consequences of an increased inventory turnover period are the costs of storing, handling and insuring inventory levels will also increase. There is also an increased risk of inventory damage and obsolescence.

An alternative calculation is to calculate inventory turnover as a number of time per annum:

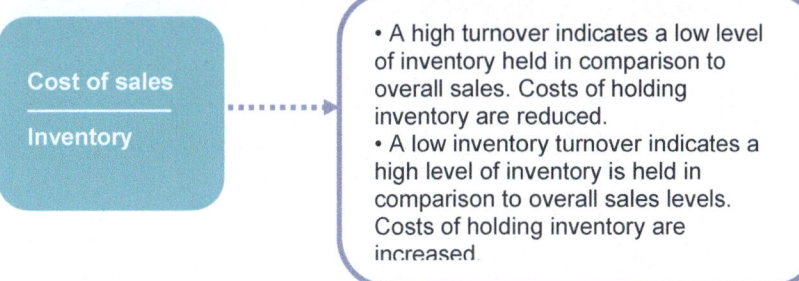

$$\frac{\text{Cost of sales}}{\text{Inventory}}$$

- A high turnover indicates a low level of inventory held in comparison to overall sales. Costs of holding inventory are reduced.
- A low inventory turnover indicates a high level of inventory is held in comparison to overall sales levels. Costs of holding inventory are increased.

Receivables collection period

It is calculated as follows:

$$\frac{\text{Trade receivables}}{\text{Credit sales}} \times 365 \text{ days}$$

Increasing receivables collection days may indicate a lack of proper credit control but can be due to:
- A significant new customer being allowed different (longer) terms.
- A deliberate policy to increase allowable credit terms to attract more trade.

The receivables days' ratio can be distorted by a number of factors:

- using year-end figures as opposed to average receivables,

- using factoring of accounts receivables figures which results in very low trade receivables,
- sales on unusually long credit terms to a select few customers which is out of the norm.

Payables collection period

The payables collection period is calculated as follows:

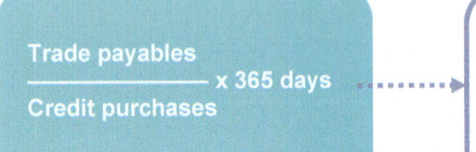

$$\frac{\text{Trade payables}}{\text{Credit purchases}} \times 365 \text{ days}$$

Increasing payables payment days may indicate:
- the company is unable to pay more quickly because of liquidity problems. A long credit period may be good as it represents a source of free finance.

KEY POINT If the credit period is long the company may develop a poor reputation as a slow payer. Existing suppliers may decide to discontinue supplies and new suppliers may not be prepared to offer credit. Also the business may be losing out on worthwhile cash discounts for prompt payment.

Cash conversion cycle

The cash conversion cycle ('CCC') can be used to determine how many days cash is tied up on the working capital cycle as follows:

Inventory holding period + receivables collection period – payables payment period.

KEY POINT Ideally, businesses would like to have cash tied up in working capital for the minimum number of days possible.

19.5 FINANCIAL POSITION RATIOS

Gearing

When assessing the financial position of a business the main focus is its stability and exposure to risk. This is typically assessed by considering the gearing.

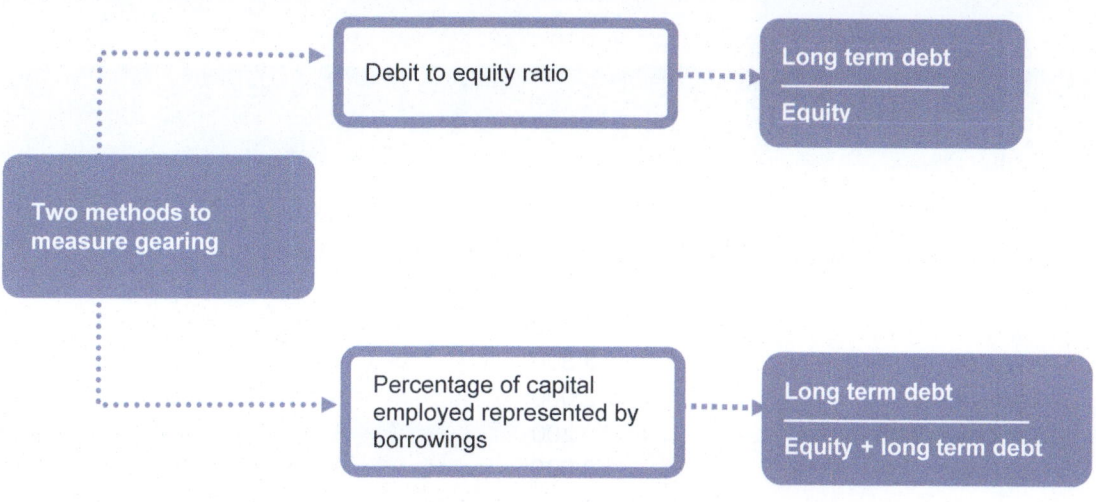

Two methods to measure gearing

Debit to equity ratio

$$\frac{\text{Long term debt}}{\text{Equity}}$$

Percentage of capital employed represented by borrowings

$$\frac{\text{Long term debt}}{\text{Equity} + \text{long term debt}}$$

KEY POINT Long term debt includes non-current loan and redeemable preference share liabilities. Equity includes share capital (and premium) balances plus reserves (revaluation reserve, retained earnings).

Interest cover

DEFINITION Interest cover indicates the ability of a company to pay interest out of profits generated.

Interest cover is calculated as follows:

$$\frac{\text{Profit before interest and tax}}{\text{Interest payable}}$$

Low levels of interest cover (less than two is deemed unsatisfactory) indicates:
• shareholders' dividends are at risk as profits are eaten up by interest payments
• the business may have difficulty financing its debts if its profits fall further.

Do you understand?

1   What are the two methods to measure gearing?

2   The trade receivables days for ABC Ltd have increased – this could be due to an increase in credit terms as an incentive to attract customers.

   True or false?

3   Why does the quick ratio exclude inventory from current assets?

4   What does net asset turnover measure?

---

1   The two methods to measure gearing are 1) debt to equity ratio and 2) percentage of capital employed represented by borrowings.

2   True.

3   Inventory is excluded from the quick ratio as it is considered to potentially be a slow moving asset so emphasis is concentrated on having sufficient liquid assets to cover current liabilities.

4   Net asset turnover measures management's efficiency in generating revenue from the net assets at its disposal.

1   B Co had the following details extracted from its statement of financial position:

	$000
Inventory	3,800
Receivables	2,000
Bank overdraft	200
Payables	2,000

What was the current ratio based upon the available information?

A   1.72:1

B   2.90:1

C   2.64:1

D   3.00:1

2   B Co had the following details extracted from its statement of financial position:

	$000
Inventory	3,800
Receivables	2,000
Bank overdraft	200
Payables	2,000

Based upon the available information, what was the quick (acid test) ratio of B Co?

A   2.63 : 1

B   0.9 : 1

C   29.0 : 1

D   1 : 1

3   **Which one of the following is likely to reduce the trade payables payment period?**

A   Offering credit customers a significant discount for prompt payment within seven days of receipt of invoice

B   Paying trade suppliers within seven days of receipt of invoice to obtain a discount

C   Buying proportionately more goods on a cash basis, rather than on a credit basis

D   Buying an increasing volume of credit purchases during an accounting period

4   On 1 July 20X5, D Co raised $5 million from an issue of ordinary shares. D Co then immediately used this cash to repay a loan of $5 million, which was not due for repayment until 30 June 20X9.

What impact did this have upon the debt/equity ratio?

A   It is not possible to determine the impact on the debt/equity ratio as there is insufficient information available

B   The debt/equity ratio increased

C   The debt/equity ratio decreased

D   There will be no change to the debt/equity ratio

20.1 WHAT CONSTITUTES A GROUP

LEARNING SUMMARY

After studying this section you should be able to:

- define and explain terms relevant to group accounting.

Control

DEFINITION A **group** exists where one entity, the **parent** (referred to as 'the **investor**'), has **control** over another entity, the **subsidiary** (referred to as 'the **investee**').

IFRS 10 specifies three criteria that must be present for control to be established:

Power over the investee, which is normally exercised through the majority of voting rights (i.e. owning more than 50% of the equity shares).

Exposure or rights to variable returns from involvement (e.g. a dividend).

The ability to use power over the investee to affect the amount of investor returns. This is regarded as a crucial determinant in deciding whether or not control is exercised (IFRS 10, para 7).

'Power' is normally regarded as the parent having the ability to direct the activities of the subsidiary that significantly affect returns that will be generated.

DEFINITION A **parent** is an entity that controls one or more entities (IFRS 10, Appendix A).

DEFINITION A **subsidiary** is an entity that is controlled by another entity (IFRS 10. Appendix A).

DEFINITION A **non-controlling interest** is 'an equity in a subsidiary not attributable, directly or indirectly, to a parent' (IFRS 10, Appendix A).

Control is normally indicated when one entity owns a majority (in excess of 50%) of the equity shares of another entity.

Remember definitions as they may be tested in the objective test part of the examination.

Single entity concept

KEY POINT If one entity controls another then IFRS 10 requires that a single set of consolidated financial statements be prepared to reflect the financial performance and position of the group as one combined entity.

20.2 PREPARING A CONSOLIDATED STATEMENT OF FINANCIAL POSITION

LEARNING SUMMARY

After studying this section you should be able to:

- prepare a consolidated statement of financial position.

The basic method of preparing a consolidated statement of financial position

1	The assets and liabilities of the parent and the subsidiary are added together on a line-by-line basis.
2	The investment in the subsidiary included in the parent's statement of financial position is replaced by a goodwill asset in the consolidated statement of financial position.
3	The share capital and share premium balances of the parent and subsidiary are not added together; only the parent entity balances for share capital and share premium are included in the consolidated statement of financial position.
4	The amount attributable to non-controlling interests is calculated and shown separately on the face of the consolidated statement of financial position.
5	The group share of the subsidiary's post-acquisition retained earnings is calculated and included as part of group retained earnings.

> This reflects the consolidated statement of financial position. It includes all assets and liabilities under the control of the parent entity.

The mechanics of consolidation

There are standard workings to follow:

Working 1 – establish group structure and date of acquisition

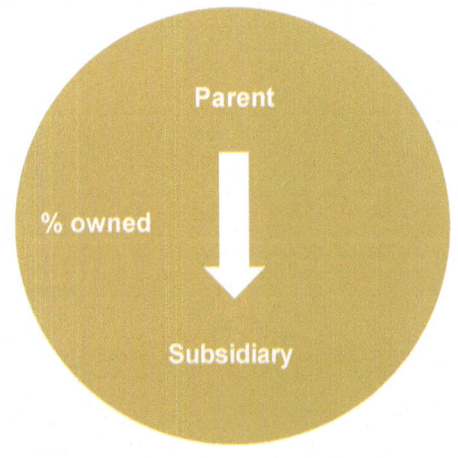

Non-controlling interest %

> The non-controlling interests represent the 'other' shareholders of the subsidiary, where the parent owns less than 100% of the ordinary shares.

Working 2 – net assets of the subsidiary

	At date of acquisition $	At reporting date $
Share capital	X	X
Share premium	X	X
Revaluation surplus	X	X
Retained earnings	X	X
	X	X

KEY POINT The total of share capital and share premium from the subsidiary statement of financial position should be unchanged at both the date of acquisition and the reporting date.

Working 3 – calculate goodwill

The value of an entity will normally exceed the value of its net assets. The difference is goodwill.

DEFINITION **Goodwill** represents assets not included in the statement of financial position of the acquired entity such as the reputation of the business, brand and the experience of employees.

Fair value (FV) of consideration paid	X
FV of non-controlling interest (NCI) at acquisition	X
	X
Less:	
FV of net assets at acquisition (W2)	(X)
Goodwill on acquisition	X

Working 4 – non-controlling interest

FV of NCI at acquisition (as in W3)	X
NCI share of post-acquisition reserves (W2)	X
	X

KEY POINT When calculating goodwill and non-controlling interests the fair value method is used. This means that amounts are not calculated merely at their reported carrying amount.

DEFINITION **Fair value** is defined as "the price that would be received to sell an asset or paid to transfer a liability in an orderly transaction between market participants at the measurement date." i.e. it is an exit price (IFRS 13, para 9).

The need to account on a fair value basis reflects the statement of financial position often valuing items (mainly non-current assets) at their historic cost less depreciation. This may mean the carrying value of those assets is significantly different to their current market values.

How to include fair values in consolidation workings:

Adjust both columns of W2 to bring the net assets to fair value at acquisition and reporting date. This will ensure that the fair value of net assets is carried through to the goodwill (W3) and non-controlling interest calculations (W4).

	At date of acquisition $	At reporting date $
Share capital	X	X
Share premium	X	X
Revaluation surplus	X	X
Retained earnings	X	X
Fair value adjustments	X	X
	X	X

Fair value adjustment

P's retained earnings (100%)	X
P's % of sub's post-acquisition retained earnings	X
	X

Intra-group trading

The parent and subsidiary may trade with each other which can lead to the following issues to be dealt with:

Receivables and payables in the parent and subsidiary accounts- which effectively cancel each other out.

Dividends paid by the subsidiary recognised as income by the parent. If a dividend is paid by one entity and received by the other, the net effect of this to the group is zero.

Unrealised profits on sales of inventory between the parent and the subsidiary

Current accounts

If the parent and the subsidiary trade with each other on credit it leads to amounts that should not be consolidated because the group would end up with a receivable to itself and a payable to itself. This would overstate receivables and payables in the group statement of financial position. Therefore, the balances are cancelled against each other on consolidation.

Unrealised profits

When one group entity sells goods to another it is not just the current accounts that must be cancelled. Other adjustments may be needed:

- Where goods are still held by one entity at the reporting date, any unrealised profit must be cancelled.

- Inventory must be included at original cost to the group.

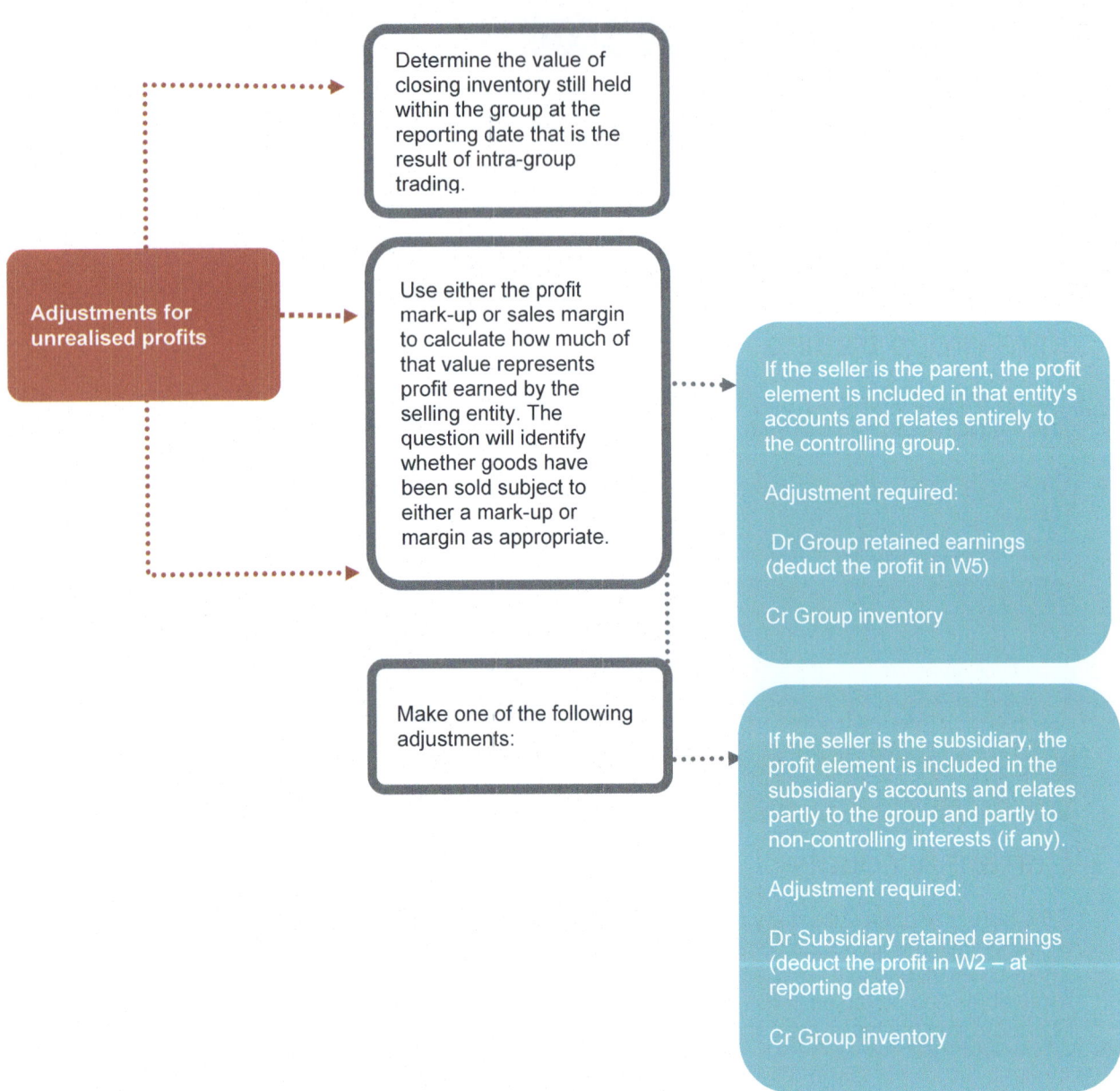

Mid-year acquisitions - Calculation of reserves at date of acquisition

If a parent entity acquires a subsidiary mid-year, the net assets must be calculated at the date of acquisition.

The net assets at acquisition can be calculated as the net assets at the start of the subsidiary's financial year plus the retained for part of the year up to the date of acquisition, together with any fair value adjustments at the date of acquisition.

To calculate this, it is normally assumed that S's profit after tax has accrued evenly throughout the year.

> Make sure you check the date of acquisition in a scenario.

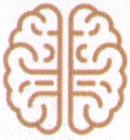

Do you understand?

1   What percentage ownership would be required for holding the majority of voting rights?

2   To prepare a consolidated statement of financial position, the assets and liabilities of the parent and the non-controlling interest are added together on a line-by-line basis.

     True or false?

3   What is the definition of goodwill?

4   What is the purpose of making fair value adjustments?

1   Owning more than 50% of the equity shares.

2   False. The assets and liabilities of the parent and the subsidiary are added together on a line-by-line basis.

3   Goodwill represents assets not included in the statement of financial position of the acquired entity such as the reputation of the business, brand and the experience of employees. The value of the entity normally exceeds the value of its net assets. The difference is goodwill.

4   The need to account on a fair value basis reflects the statement of financial position often valuing items (mainly non-current assets) at their historic cost less depreciation. This may mean the carrying value of those assets is significantly different to their current market values.

1   At 1 January 20X8 Tom acquired 80% of the share capital of Jerry for $100,000. At that date the share capital of Jerry consisted of 50,000 ordinary shares of $1 each and its reserves were $30,000. At 31 December 20X9 the reserves of Tom and Jerry were as follows:

Tom $400,000

Jerry $50,000

In the consolidated statement of financial position of Tom and its subsidiary Jerry at 31 December 20X9, what amount should appear for group reserves?

A $400,000

B $438,000

C $416,000

D $404,000

2   At 1 January 20X6 Gary acquired 60% of the share capital of Barlow for $35,000. At that date the share capital of Barlow consisted of 20,000 ordinary shares of $1 each and its reserves were $10,000. At 31 December 20X9 the reserves of Gary and Barlow were as follows:

Gary $40,000

Barlow $15,000

At the date of acquisition the fair value of the non-controlling interest was valued at $25,000.

In the consolidated statement of financial position of Gary and its subsidiary Barlow at 31 December 20X9, what amount should appear for non-controlling interest?

A $25,000

B $27,000

C $28,000

D $31,000

3   Salt owns 70% of Pepper and sells goods to Pepper valued at $1,044 at a mark-up of 20%. 40% of these goods were sold on by Pepper to external parties at the year end.

What is the provision for unrealised profit (PURP) adjustment in the group financial statements?

A $69.60

B $104.40

C $125.28

D $83.52

4   **Which of the following would normally indicate that one entity has control over the activities of another?**

A   Ownership of some equity shares in another entity

B   Ownership of up to twenty per cent of the equity shares of another entity

C   Ownership of over fifty per cent of the equity shares of another entity

D   Ownership of between twenty per cent and fifty per cent of the equity shares of another entity

5   **The statements of financial position for Pebble and Stone as at 31 December 20X6 are presented below:**

Assets	Pebble	Stone
Non-current assets	$	$
Property, plant and equipment	300,000	225,000
Investments	400,000	–
Current assets		
Inventories	80,000	75,000
Trade and other receivables	60,000	140,000
Cash and cash equivalents	10,000	25,000
Total assets	850,000	465,000
Equity and liabilities		
Equity		
Share capital	80,000	60,000
Share premium	20,000	10,000
Retained earnings	295,000	250,000
Non-current liabilities		
Loans	300,000	85,000
Current liabilities		
Trade and other payables	155,000	60,000
Total equity and liabilities	850,000	465,000

The following notes are relevant to the preparation of the consolidated financial statements:

(i)   Pebble acquired 80% of the ordinary shares of Stone for $400,000 on 1 January 20X2. At the acquisition date, the retained earnings of Stone were $150,000. The fair value of the non-controlling interest in Stone at the date of acquisition was $80,000.

(ii)   At the date of acquisition, the fair values of the net assets of Stone approximated their carrying amounts, with the exception of a plot of land owned by Stone. This land was held in the financial statements of Stone at its cost of $150,000 but was estimated to have a fair value of $180,000. This land was still owned by Stone at 31 December 20X6.

(iii)   During the year, Pebble sold goods to Stone for $50,000 making a gross profit margin on the sale of 25%. Two fifths of these goods are still included in the inventories of Stone at 31 December 20X6.

Required:

(a) Prepare the consolidated statement of financial position for the Pebble group as at 31 December 20X6.

(b) Pebble is considering making an investment in another entity, Archive, which would be accounted for as an associate. Which TWO of the following factors would be relevant when accounting for an associate?

- Control of Archive

- Significant influence in Archive

- Owning the majority of the ordinary shares of Archive

- Owning between 20% and 50% of the ordinary shares of Archive

- Accounting for goodwill

- Accounting of non-controlling interests.

> This question involves associates which are covered in the next chapter.

21 **Consolidated statement of profit or loss and associates**

The following topics are covered in this chapter:
- Preparing a consolidated statement of profit or loss
- Accounting for investments in associates

21.1 PREPARING A CONSOLIDATED STATEMENT OF PROFIT OR LOSS

LEARNING SUMMARY

After studying this section you should be able to:
- prepare a consolidated statement of profit or loss

KEY POINT The consolidated statement of profit or loss follows the same basic principles as the consolidated statement of financial position.

The basic method of preparing a consolidated statement of profit or loss

1	Add together the revenues and expenses of the parent and the subsidiary.
2	Eliminate intra-group sales and purchases.
3	Eliminate unrealised profit held in closing inventory relating to intragroup trading.
4	Calculate the profits attributable to the non-controlling interests. After profit for the year, show the split of profit between amounts attributable to the parent's shareholders and the non-controlling interest (to reflect ownership).

If the subsidiary is acquired part-way through the year, revenues and expenses of the subsidiary must be time apportioned. during the consolidation process.

Non-controlling interest

	$
NCI % × subsidiary's profit after tax	X
Less: NCI % × PURP (when the sub is the seller only)	(X)
	X

Intra-group trading

KEY POINT The effect of intra-group trading must be eliminated from the consolidated statement of profit or loss.

- Consolidated sales revenue = P's revenue + S's revenue – intra-group sales.

- Consolidated cost of sales = P's COS + S's COS – intra-group purchases.

Provisions for unrealised profits

KEY POINT If any goods traded between the parent and the subsidiary are included in closing inventory, their value must be adjusted to the lower of cost and net realisable value (NRV) to the group (as in the consolidated statement of financial position).

The adjustment for unrealised profit should be shown as an increase to cost of sales (return inventory back to true cost to group and eliminate unrealised profit).

Mid-year acquisitions

KEY POINT If a subsidiary was acquired part way through the year, the subsidiary's results should be consolidated from the date of acquisition, i.e. the date when control was acquired.

21.2 ACCOUNTING FOR INVESTMENTS

LEARNING SUMMARY

After studying this section you should be able to:

- understand how to account for investments in associates

- describe the principle of equity accounting.

Results of the subsidiary in the year of acquisition will be time apportioned. After time-apportioning the results, deduct post-acquisition intra-group items as normal.

Associates

DEFINITION An **associate** is defined as 'an entity over which the investor has significant influence' (IFRS 28, para 3).

DEFINITION **Significant influence** is 'the power to participate in the financial and operating policy decisions of the investee but is not control or joint control over those policies' (IAS 28, para 3).

Joint ventures are not part of the syllabus for this paper.

KEY POINT An investor is presumed to have significant influence over another entity when it has a shareholding in that other entity between 20% and 50%.

Equity accounting

DEFINITION **Equity accounting** is a method of accounting where the investment is initially recorded at cost and adjusted thereafter for the post-acquisition change in the investor's share of net assets of the associate.

The effect of this is summarised for both the consolidated statement of financial position and consolidated statement of profit or loss:

Equity accounting in the consolidated statement of financial position	Equity accounting in the consolidated statement of profit or loss
100% of the assets and liabilities of the parent and subsidiary entity on a line-by-line basis.	100% of the income and expenses of the parent and subsidiary entity on a line-by-line basis .
A single 'investments in associates' line within non-current assets which includes the group share of the assets and liabilities of any associate.	A single 'share of profit of associates' line which includes the group share of any associate's profit after tax.

Associates in the statement of financial position

The consolidated statement of financial position is prepared on a normal line-by-line basis following the acquisition method for the parent and subsidiary.

The associate is included as a one-line item as a non-current asset investment, calculated as follows:

	$
Cost of investment	X
Share of post-acquisition profits	X
Less:	
Impairment losses	(X)
Group share of provision for unrealised profit (parent = seller)	(X)
	X

Associates in the statement of profit or loss

The equity method of accounting requires that the consolidated statement of profit or loss:

- does not include dividends from the associate

- includes the group share of the associate's profit after tax less any impairment of the associate in the year (included after group profit from operations in arriving at the group profit before tax in the consolidated statement of profit or loss).

Trading with the associate

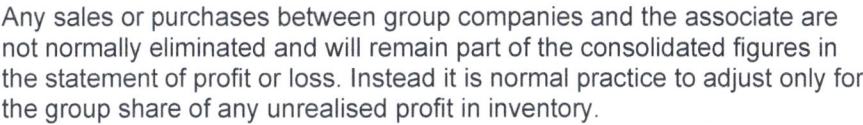

Any sales or purchases between group companies and the associate are not normally eliminated and will remain part of the consolidated figures in the statement of profit or loss. Instead it is normal practice to adjust only for the group share of any unrealised profit in inventory.

Do you understand?

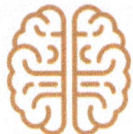

1   What is equity accounting?

2   What percentage ownership is considered to be a 'significant influence'?

3   Are intra-group sales added or deducted from the group sales revenue figure?

1   Equity accounting is a method of accounting where the investment is initially recorded at cost and adjusted thereafter for the post-acquisition change in the investor's share of net assets of the associate.

2   An investor is presumed to have significant influence over another entity when it has a shareholding in that other entity between 20% and 50%.

3   Intra-group sales are deducted from the group sales revenue figure.

1   Spice owns 70% of Paprika and sells goods to Paprika valued at
    $1,044 at a mark-up of 20%. 40% of these goods were sold on by
    Paprika to external parties at the year end.

    **What is the provision for unrealised profit (PURP) adjustment in
    the group financial statements?**

    A $69.60

    B $104.40

    C $125.28

    D $83.52

2   Entity X acquired sixty per cent of the issued equity shares of entity Z
    on 1 October 20X3. During the year ended 31 December 20X3, X and
    Z had sales revenue of $2 million and $1.5 million respectively.
    During the post-acquisition period, X made sales to Z of $0.1 million.

    **What is the group sales revenue figure for the year ended 31
    December 20X3?**

    A $2.275 million

    B $2.375 million

    C $3.4 million

    D $3.5 million

3   On 1 June 20X6 Chuck acquired control of Axelrod. During the year
    ended 30 September 20X6, Chuck and Axelrod had cost of sales of
    $10 million and $6 million respectively. During the post-acquisition
    period, Chuck had sales to Axelrod of $1.8 million. These sales had
    been made at a mark-up of twenty per cent and at the year end, one
    third of the goods remained within Axelrod's inventory.

    **What was the group cost of sales figure for the year ended 30
    September 20X6?**

4   On 1 July 20X5 Hopper acquired sixty per cent of the equity shares of
    Sooty. For the year ended 31 December 20X5, Hopper made a profit
    after tax of $600,000 and Sooty had a profit after tax of $400,000.
    During the post-acquisition period, Hopper sold goods to Sooty which
    included a profit element of $20,000. At the year-end, one quarter of
    the goods sold by Hopper to Sooty remained within the inventory of
    Sooty.

    **What was the non-controlling interest share of the group profit
    after tax for the year ended 31 December 20X5?**

    A $75,000

    B $80,000

    C $120,000

    D $160,000

5 The following statements of profit or loss relate to Helsinki and its subsidiary Stockholm for the year ended 31 December 20X6:

	Helsinki $000	Stockholm $000
Revenue	200,000	100,000
Cost of sales	(110,000)	(50,000)
Gross profit	90,000	50,000
Distribution costs	(20,000)	(10,000)
Administrative expenses	(40,000)	(20,000)
Operating profit	30,000	20,000
Investment income from Stockholm	7,500	
Profit before tax	37,500	20,000
Taxation	(10,500)	(6,000)
Profit for the year	27,000	14,000

The following notes are relevant to the preparation of the consolidated financial statements:

(i) Helsinki acquired three million of the equity shares of Stockholm on 30 June 20X6 when Stockholm had a total of four million equity shares in issue. Helsinki paid a total of $25 million to acquire the shares.

(ii) At 30 June 20X6, the retained earnings of Stockholm were $20 million and the carrying amounts of the net assets of Stockholm approximated to their fair values.

(iii) It is group accounting policy to account for non-controlling interest at its fair value. At the date of acquisition, the fair value of the non-controlling interest in Stockholm was $7 million.

(iv) During the post-acquisition period, Stockholm sold goods to Helsinki. The goods originally cost $10 million and they were sold to Helsinki at a mark-up of 25%. At 31 December 20X6, Helsinki still had 40% of these goods within its inventory.

Required:

(a) Calculate goodwill arising on acquisition of Stockholm by Helsinki.

(b) Prepare the consolidated statement of profit or loss for the Helsinki group for the year ended 31 December 20X6.

CHAPTER 1

1   C

2   C

3   D

All of the remaining answers include only part of the full definition of an asset.

4   C

5   **B and D**

The remaining answers are fundamental qualitative characteristics of useful financial information.

CHAPTER 2

1   C

2   B

The Framework is not an accounting standard itself, although it is used as a reference document when new standards are developed.

3   B

CHAPTER 3

1   C

2   D

An invoice is raised by a business and issued to a customer. It contains more than the amount due to be paid for goods and services supplied. It will also include the quantity and description of goods, the date of supply and the net amount, sales tax applied and gross amount due.

3   C

The journal records all transactions not already recorded in a book of prime entry. Bank and cash transactions are recorded in the cash book and petty cash book respectively. Credit sales transactions are recorded in the sales day book.

4   C

Books of prime entry include: sales day book, purchases day book, sales returns day book, purchases returns day book, cash book, petty cash book and the journal.

5   A

CHAPTER 4

1   C

2   D

3

Element	Statement of profit or loss	Statement of financial position
Assets		✓
Liabilities		✓
Expenses	✓	
Income	✓	
Equity		✓

4

	Debit	Credit
Increases in capital/equity		✓
Increase in assets	✓	
Decreases in assets		✓
Increases in income		✓
Increases in expenses	✓	

CHAPTER 5

1   C

The receivables account should be credited with the full amount of the sales return, including the sales tax. The sales returns (returns inwards) should be debited with the value of the returns excluding the sales tax. The sales tax account should be debited with the amount of tax on the returns (as the output tax will no longer be payable).

2

	Ledger Account:	$
Debit	Receivables	12,000
Credit	Sales	10,000
Credit	Sales tax	2,000

3

	Ledger Account:	$
Debit	Purchases (100/115 × $1,541)	1,340
Debit	Sales tax (15/115 × $1,541)	201
Credit	Payables	1,541

4 $655.50

	$
Price	600.00
Less: trade discount (5% × $600)	(30.00)
	570.00
Add: sales tax at 15% (15% × $570)	85.50
	655.50

5   C

	$
Sales net of sales tax	90,000
Purchases net of sales tax	(72,000)
	18,000
Tax payable @ 10%	$1,800

As sales exceed purchases, the excess sales tax is payable to the tax authorities.

6 $5,300

Sales tax

	$		$
Tax on purchases	6,000	Balance b/f	3,400
Bank	2,600	Tax on sales	10,500
Balance c/f	5,300		
	13,900		13,900
		Balance b/f	5,300

Tax on sales (outputs) = 17.5% × $60,000 = $10,500

Tax on purchases (inputs) = (17.5/117.5) × $40,286 = $6,000

CHAPTER 6

1 $4,700

	Net realisable value	Lower of cost or NRV	Units	Value
	$	$		$
B2	8	6	200	1,200
S1	8	8	250	2,000
L3	10	10	150	1,500
Total value				4,700

2   B

At the year-end:

1   Opening inventory must be removed from the statement of financial position inventory account (a credit) and expensed to the statement of profit or loss as part of cost of sales (a debit).

2   Closing inventory must be debited on to the statement of financial position as an asset and removed from the cost of sales (a credit).

3   B

• If prices have fallen during the year, AVCO will give a higher value of closing inventory than FIFO, which values goods for resale at the latest prices.

• Where the value of closing inventory is higher, profits are higher.

4 $500

• The inventory should be valued at the lower of cost and NRV.

• Cost is $500.

• NRV is $1,200 – $250 = $950.

• The correct valuation is therefore $500.

CHAPTER 7

1 $86,000

	$
Purchase cost of machine	80,000
Installation	5,000
Pre-production safety testing	1,000
	86,000

A non-current asset should be measured initially at its cost. 'Cost' means the amounts incurred to acquire the asset and bring it into working condition for its intended use. These include the purchase cost, initial delivery and handling costs, installation costs and professional fees. Costs of testing whether the asset is working properly may be included, but staff training costs cannot be capitalised.

2   D

Painting and replacing windows are maintenance and repairs, and so are classified as 'revenue expenditure' and must be expensed through the statement of profit or loss. The purchase of a car for resale means that the car is an item of inventory for the business, not a non-current asset. Legal fees incurred in purchasing a building are included in the cost of the building, and therefore are part of the non-current asset cost, i.e. capital expenditure.

3   C

4   D

The reducing balance method charges more depreciation in earlier years than in later years. It is therefore appropriate to use for assets such as motor vehicles that lose a large part of their value in the earlier years of their life.

CHAPTER 8

1   C

Asset register

Carrying amount per question	$85,600
Addition of land	$30,000
	$115,600

Ledger accounts

Carrying amount per question	$130,000
Disposal at carrying amount	($14,400)
	$115,600

2   A

		$
1.1.X4	Cost	235,000
	Depreciation at 30%	(70,500)
y/e 31.12.X4	Carrying amount	164,500
	Depreciation at 30%	(49,350)
y/e 31.12.X5	Carrying amount	115,150
	Depreciation at 30%	(34,545)
	Carrying amount	80,605
	Accumulated depreciation	
	(70,500 + 49,350 + 34,545)	154,395

Therefore Uplift cost account to valuation

Dr Cost $65,000

(1)   Remove depreciation to date

Dr Accumulated depreciation $154,395

(2)   Send the balance to the revaluation surplus

Cr Revaluation surplus $219,395

3   D

A non-current asset register is a detailed schedule of non-current assets, and is not another name for non-current asset ledger accounts in the general ledger.

4 $192,600

Depreciation on additions: 20% × $48,000 × 6/12 =	$4,800
Depreciation on disposals: 20% × $84,000 × 9/12 =	$12,600
Depreciation on other assets: 20% × (960,000 − 84,000) =	$175,200
	$192,600

CHAPTER 9

1　C

2　B

Answer (A) is not precise enough – there must be an annual impairment review to ensure that the asset is not overstated in the financial statements.

3　A

An intangible asset may be internally generated (development costs per IAS 38) and may also be purchased – therefore answers B and D are incorrect. Answer C is incorrect as assets can normally be sold.

4　A, C and D.

CHAPTER 10

1　B

The charge in the statement of profit or loss will be the amount of interest incurred from 1 January (when the loan was taken out) to 30 September (the year-end) i.e. 9/12 × 12% × $100,000 = $9,000. This represents three interest payments. However, as only two interest payments were made (1 April and 1 July) the third payment due to be made on 1 October, which relates to the three months to 30 September, will be accrued: 3/12 × 12% × $100,000 = $3,000.

2　D

Statement of profit or loss:

(5/12 × $24,000) + (7/12 × $30,000) = $27,500

Statement of financial position:

$7,500 paid on 1 January therefore amount prepaid by tenant is:

2/3 × $7,500 = $5,000. For Lamb Ltd this is prepaid income, i.e. income received in advance – a liability.

3　**$385**

Motor expenses

	$		$
Balance b/f (insurance)	80	Balance b/f (fuel)	95
Cash paid – petrol	95		
– other bills	245	**SPL (β)**	**385**
Balance c/f (petrol)	120	Balance c/f (insurance)	60
	———		———
	540		540
	———		———

The insurance prepayment covers 4 months as at the start of September. Therefore there must be a prepayment of 3 months at the end of September.

CHAPTER 11

1   A

		Allowance	Expense
	$	$	$
Receivables balance (draft)	58,200		
Irrecoverable debts	(8,900)		8,900
	49,300		
Specific allowance: Carroll	(1,350)	1,350	
Juffs	(750)	750	
Mary	(1,416)	1,416	
Allowance c/f		3,516	
Allowance b/f		5,650	
Decrease in allowance		2,134	(2,134)

Total expense = $8,900 − $2,134 = $6,766

2   A

Year-end receivables 5% × $7,000,000 =	$350,000
Year-end allowance for receivables 4% × $350,000 =	$14,000
Allowance at start of year 100/120 × $14,000 =	$11,667
Increase in allowance =	$2,333

Irrecoverable debts expense

	$		$
Write off of irrecoverable debts	3,200	Recovery of irrecoverable debts	450
Increase in allowance	2,333	Statement of profit or loss (β)	5,083
	5,533		5,533

3   C

When a debt is written off as irrecoverable, the transaction is recorded as:

Debit   Irrecoverable debts account

Credit   Receivables

Any subsequent change to the allowance for receivables should be dealt with as a separate matter.

CHAPTER 12

1 A

    (i)   Based upon the stated and publicised policy it would appear probable that customers who return goods in accordance with the policy will expect to receive a refund and so this requires a provision.

    (ii)   The outcome of the legal claim has been assessed as only possible (rather than probable) that there will be an outflow of economic benefits. This does not require a provision, only a disclosure note of the contingent liability.

2 A

3 D

IAS 37 requires that a provision should be recognised when it is probable that there will be a future outflow of economic benefits as a result of a past event. Therefore, a provision to settle customer claims should be recognised. As it is only probable that the counter-claim against Jasmine Co will succeed, it cannot be recognised in the statement of financial position – it is disclosed in a note to the financial statements.

CHAPTER 13

1 A and D

2

Debit or credit	Ledger account	$
Debit	Bank (20,000 × $1.75)	35,000
Credit	Share capital ($20,000 × $1)	20,000
Credit	Share premium ($20,000 × $0.75)	15,000

3 B

The accounting entries would be:

Dr Share premium $31,250

Cr Share capital (250,000/4) = 62,500 × $0.50 = $31,250

4 B

The profit or loss charge would be $500 under-provision brought forward from last year plus the charge for the current year of $8,000 = $8,500.

The liability outstanding would be $8,000.

CHAPTER 14

1   **D**

Cash book	$	
Cash book balance per question	(1,350)	Credit therefore overdrawn
Standing order not yet recorded	(300)	
	———	
Revised cash book balance	(1,650)	
	———	

	$
Balance per bank statement (β)	(1,707)
Unpresented cheques	(56)
Uncleared lodgements	128
Bank error	(15)
	———
Revised balance = cash book balance	(1,650)
	———

On the bank statement the overdrawn balance is shown as a debit (i.e. from the bank's perspective they are owed money).

2   **C**

Item 1 – unpresented cheques are those issued by a business but not yet banked by the recipient. They should be deducted from the balance shown on the bank statement in order to reflect the true bank balance.

Item 2 – a dishonoured cheque is recorded by crediting the cash book. The cheque would previously have been debited to cash when received. The credit is the reversal of that entry.

Item 3 – a bank error should be corrected by amendment to the balance per the bank statement.

Item 4 – from the bank's perspective an overdraft means that they are owed money by the customer. Hence it is shown as a debit (an asset to the bank) in the bank statement.

3   **B**

Cash

	$		$
Draft balance	2,490		
		Bank charges	50
		Dishonoured cheque	140
		Revised balance	2,300
	———		———
	2,490		2,490
	———		———

4   **B**

PLCA

	$
Draft balance	768,420
Reverse incorrect debit entry	28,400
Discounts received – correct entry	(15,620)
	———
Revised balance	781,200
	———

Payables ledger

$

Draft balance	781,200
	———
	781,200
	———

Items A and D would explain the discrepancy if the balance on the control account was $12,780 greater than the balance on the payables ledger.

Item C would explain the balance on the payables ledger being $25,560 greater than the balance on the control account.

5   D

	SLCA
	$
Draft balance per question	37,642
Correction of misposted contra	(1,802)
	———
Revised balance = receivables ledger balance	35,840
	———

The balance on the control account exceeds the total of the individual account balances by $1,802. Items A, B and C would all have the effect of making the total of the individual account balances higher by $1,802. Item D, however, by recording a credit item as a debit item in the control account, has made the control account debit balance too high by $901 × 2 = $1,802.

CHAPTER 15

1   C

All three are limitations of a trial balance:

- figures in the trial balance are not necessarily the final figures to be reported in the financial statements; they are subject to year-end adjustments

- errors of commission (where an entry has been posted to the wrong account) are not identified by the trial balance since an equal debit and credit entry are still posted

- although a trial balance can identify if double entry has broken down, it does not indicate in which accounts wrong entries were made.

2   C and D

3   A

Suspense account

	$		$
Imbalance on TB (362,350 – 347,800)	14,550		
Disposals (2)	9,000		
Allowance for receivables (3)	2,600	Balance c/f	26,150
	——		——
	26,150		26,150
	——		——
Balance b/f	26,150		

The suspense account is only affected where the initial debit and credit were unequal:

(1)   An incorrect entry into the sales day book means that the subtotal of the day book is wrong and both sides of the double entry have been made for the wrong amount. This does not affect the suspense account.

(2)   An unequal entry has occurred:

$

Entry was:	Dr Cash	9,000
	(Cr Suspense	9,000)
To correct:	Dr Suspense	9,000
	Cr Disposals	9,000

> **KEY POINT** Don't worry about the other journals required to record the disposal – they have not been recorded at all and so do not affect the suspense account.

(3)   An unequal entry has occurred:

Entry was:	Dr Irrecoverable debt expense	1,300
	Dr Allowance for receivables	1,300
	(Cr Suspense	2,600)
To correct:	Dr Suspense	2,600
	Cr Allowance for receivables	2,600

CHAPTER 16

1   B

	$	$
Sales (β)		25,600
Cost of sales		
Opening inventory	1,500	
Purchases	12,950	
Inventory drawings	(75)	
Closing inventory	(900)	
	——	
		(13,475)
		——
Gross profit		12,125
		——

2   C

	Cost of sales $	Administrative expense $	Distribution costs $
Opening inventory	12,500		
Closing inventory	(17,900)		
Purchases	199,000		
Distribution costs			35,600
Administrative expenses		78,800	
Audit fee		15,200	
Carriage in	3,500		
Carriage out			7,700
Depreciation (70:30:0)	28,000	12,000	
	225,100	106,000	43,300

3   D

Only dividend income is shown in the statement of profit or loss and other comprehensive income.

Only dividends payable in respect of preference shares are shown in the statement of financial position.

The statement of cash flows includes all dividends paid.

The statement of changes in equity includes dividends paid and dividends payable.

4

> **KEY POINT** Remember that, although it may be tempting to do a lot of work on your calculator, you should also include your workings as part of your submitted answers so that the marker can see what you have done. If you are not completely correct with your workings, you will be given credit for appropriate method, but the marker can only do this is they can see and understand what you have done.

Statement of profit or loss and other comprehensive income for the year ended 30 June 20X1

	$000	Marks
Revenue	100,926	0.5
Cost of sales *(Refer to W1 for cost of sales)*	(67,051)	1.5
Gross profit	33,875	
Distribution costs *(Refer to W2 for dist co)*	(7,826)	1.0
Administrative expenses *(Refer to W3 for admin expenses)*	(11,761)	1.0
Profit from operations	14,288	
Finance costs *(Refer to W4 for finance costs)*	(1,000)	1.0
Profit before taxation	13,288	
Income tax expense	(2,700)	1.0
Profit for the year	10,588	
Other comprehensive income for the year		
Surplus on revaluation of land *(Refer to W5 for revaluation)*	14,000	1.0
Total comprehensive income for the year	24,588	7.0

Statement of financial position as at 30 June 20X1

	$000	
Non-current assets		
Property, plant and equipment	119,500	2.0
Current assets		
Inventories	9,420	0.5
Trade and other receivables	20,800	1.0
Cash and cash equivalents	2,213	0.5
	————	
Total assets	151,933	
	————	
Equity		
Share capital	50,000	0.5
Share premium	25,000	0.5
Retained earnings	20,508	
Revaluation reserve ($10,000 + $14,000)	24,000	1.0
Non-current liabilities		
5% bank loan	20,000	0.5
Current liabilities		
Trade and other payables	9,725	1.0
Tax payable	2,700	0.5
	————	———
Equity and liabilities	151,933	8.0
	————	———

Refer to W6 for PPE

Refer to W7 for receivables

Refer to W5 for revaluation

Refer to W9 for payables

Refer to W8 for retained earnings

Workings

(W1) Cost of sales

	$000
Opening inventories	7,280
Purchases	67,231
Less closing inventories	(9,420)
Dep'n P&M ($2,800 × 70%)	1,960
	————
Total	67,051
	————

(W2) Distribution costs

	$000
Distribution costs	8,326
Dep'n P&M ($2,800 × 20%)	560
Advertising prepayment ($2,120 × 6/12)	(1,060)
	————
Total	7,826
	————

(W3) Administrative expenses

	$000
Administrative expenses	7,741
Depreciation Buildings	3,200
Dep'n P&M ($2,800 × 10%)	280
Irrecoverable debt	540
	————
Total	11,761
	————

(W4) Finance costs

	$000
Finance costs	0
Accrual for loan interest ($20,000 × 5%)	1,000
Total	1,000

(W5) Revaluation

	$000
Revalued amount	54,000
CV	40,000
Revaluation gain	14,000

(W6) PPE

	$000
Land and buildings cost	120,000
Revaluation	14,000
Accumulated depreciation	(22,500)
Depreciation charge (($120,000 − $40,000) × 4%)	(3,200)
Plant and equipment cost	32,000
Accumulated depreciation	(18,000)
Depreciation charge ($32,000 − $18,000) × 20%)	(2,800)
Total	119,500

(W7) Trade and other receivables

	$000
Trade and other receivables	20,280
Irrecoverable debt w/off	(540)
Advertising prepayment	1,060
Total	20,800

(W8) Retained earnings

	$000
Retained earnings	12,920
Profit per P/L	10,588
Dividends	(3,000)
Total	20,508

(W9) Trade and other payables

	$000
Trade and other payables	8,725
Accrual for loan interest	1,000
Total	9,725

CHAPTER 17

1   C

Cash

	$		$
Balance b/f	300	Bankings	50,000
Proceeds of sale of car	5,000	Wages	12,000
Sales (β)	**81,100**	Drawings	24,000
		Balance c/f	400
	86,400		86,400

2   B

	$	$	%
Sales (174,825 – 1,146)		173,679	125%
Cost of goods sold			
Opening inventory	12,274		
Purchases (136,527 – 1,084)	135,443		
Closing inventory (β)	**(8,774)**		
$173,679 × 100/125		(138,943)	100%
Gross profit		34,736	25%

3   D

	$	$	%
Sales		630,000	140
Cost of sales			
Opening Inventory	24,300		
Purchases (β)	458,450		
Closing Inventory	(32,750)		
100/140 × $630,000		(450,000)	100
		180,000	40

Payables ledger control account

	$		$
		Balance b/f	29,780
Cash paid to suppliers (β)	**453,630**	Purchases (cash and credit)	458,450
Balance c/f	34,600		
	488,230		488,230

4   B

Closing net assets	=	Opening net assets	+	Capital injections	–	Loss for the period	–	Drawings
($56,000 – $18,750)		($40,000 – $14,600)						($6,800 + $250)
$37,250	=	$25,400	+	$20,000	–	(β) **$1,100**	–	$7,050

CHAPTER 18

1   A   **False**

     B   **True**

     C   **True**

     D   **False**

2

	$
Issue of shares (560,000 – 220,000)	340,000
Issue of loan notes	300,000
	640,000

Interest paid is included within the 'operating activities' heading of the cash flow statement.

3   **C**

	$
Profit	8,000
Add: depreciation (not a cash expense)	12,000
Less: purchase of new non-current assets	(25,000)
Fall in cash balance	(5,000)

4   **D**

Items added include the depreciation charge for the period, any losses on disposals of non-current assets, reductions in inventories and receivables (including prepayments) and any increase in trade payables (including accruals).

5

KEY POINT Ensure that you remember the proforma presentation of a statement of cash flows – it will help you to complete relevant extracts in an examination question.

Firework – Statement of cash flows for the year ended 31 March 20X1

	$000	$000	Marks
Cash flows from operating activities			
Profit before tax	31,000		
Adjustments for:			
Depreciation charge	15,000		0.5
Loss on sale of plant and equipment	2,000		0.5
Interest payable	750		0.5
Increase in inventories ($36,000 – $30,000)	(6,000)		1.0
Increase in trade receivables ($40,000 – $35,000)	(5,000)		1.0
Increase in trade payables ($36,500 – $30,000)	6,500		1.0
Cash generated from operations	44,250		
Interest paid	(750)		0.5
Income taxes paid	(9,500)	34,000	1.0

Refer to W3 for income taxes paid

Refer to W2 for disposal proceeds

Refer to W4 for bank loan

Refer to W6 for dividends paid

Cash flows from investing activities

Cash purchase of property, plant and equipment	(40,000)		1.0
Disposal proceeds of plant and equipment	8,000	(32,000)	1.0

Cash flows from financing activities

Repayment of bank loan	(10,000)		1.0
Proceeds of share issue ($5,000 + $5,000)	10,000		2.0
Dividend paid	(14,000)	(14,000)	2.0

Increase in cash and cash equivalents ($10,000 + $2,000)		(12,000)	1.0
Cash and cash equivalents b/fwd		10,000	0.5
Cash and cash equivalents c/fwd (overdraft)		(2,000)	0.5
			15.0

Refer to W1 for PPE

Refer to W5 for share issues

Workings

(W1) PPE additions in the year

	$000
PPE CV bal b/fwd	93,000
Less: CV of disposals ($8,000 + $2,000 loss)	(10,000)
Less: depreciation charge	**(15,000)**
Revaluation in year	2,000
Cash paid for PPE additions	**40,000**
PPE CV bal c/fwd	110,000

(W2) Loss on disposal of plant and equipment

	$000
PPE CV of disposals ($8,000 + $2,000)	10,000
Less: loss on disposal in cost of sales	**(2,000)**
Disposal proceeds received	8,000

(W3) Income tax paid

	$000
Income tax liability b/fwd	10,000
Income tax charge for the year per P/L	6,000
Cash paid in year	**(9,500)**
Income tax liability c/fwd	6,500

(W4) Bank loan – amount repaid

	$000
Bank loan b/fwd	17,000
Cash paid	**(10,000)**
Bank loan c/fwd	7,000

(W5)   Issue of shares in the year

	Share capital $000	Share premium $000
Balance b/fwd	15,000	3,000
Proceeds of share issue in year	**5,000**	**5,000**
Balance c/fwd	20,000	8,000

(W6)   Dividend paid

	$000
Retained earnings b/fwd	85,000
Profit after tax for the year	25,000
Cash paid	**(14,000)**
Bank loan c/fwd	96,000

CHAPTER 19

1   C

The current ratio is current assets divided by current liabilities: 5,800/2,200 = 2.64:1.

2   B

The quick ratio is: current assets less inventory divided by current liabilities, which is 2,000:2,200 = 0.9:1.

3   B

Prompt payment of suppliers' invoices will reduce the trade payables payment period. Buying proportionately more, or proportionately fewer, goods on credit will not affect calculation of the trade payables payment period. Offering a discount to credit customers will not affect the trade payables payment period.

4   C

An issue of ordinary shares will increase equity, and the repayment of a non-current liability loan will decrease +-liabilities. These two factors will combine to reduce the debt/equity ratio.

CHAPTER 20

1   C

	$
Reserves of Tom	400,000
Post-acquisition reserves of Jerry – ($20,000 × 80%)	16,000
	416,000

2   B

		$
FV of NCI @ acquisition		25,000
Post-acquisition reserves of Barlow		2,000
(15,000 – 10,000) × 40%		
		———
		27,000
		———

3   B

	$	
Sales value	1,044	120%
Cost value	870	100%
	———	———
Profit	174	20%
	———	———

Workings:

Mark-up means profit is based on cost, therefore cost represents 100%. If profit is 20%, the sales value must be worth 120%.

Total profit is $174 and 60% is still in stock = $104.40

4   C

The ability of one entity to exercise control over another is normally indicated by the ability to appoint the majority of the board of directors of that other entity. Significant influence over another is normally indicated by the ability to appoint at least one director to the board of that entity.

5   Answer

(a)   Consolidated statement of financial position at 31 December 20X6

	$
Assets	
Non-current assets	
Property, plant & equip't ($300,000 + $225,000 + $30,000 FV adj)	555,000
Goodwill	230,000
Current assets	
Inventories ($80,000 + $75,000 – $5,000 PURP)	150,000
Trade and other receivables ($60,000 + $140,000)	200,000
Cash and cash equivalents ($10,000 + $25,000)	35,000
	———
Total assets	1,170,000
	———
Equity and liabilities	
Equity	
Share capital	80,000
Share premium	20,000
Retained earnings (W5)	370,000
Non-controlling interest (W4)	100,000
	———
Total equity of the group	570,000
Non-current liabilities	
Loans ($300,000 + $85,000)	385,000
Current liabilities	
Trade and other payables ($155,000 + $60,000)	215,000
	———
Total equity and liabilities	1,170,000
	———

Refer to W3 for goodwill

Refer to W6 for PURP

Refer to W5 for retained earnings

Refer to W4 for NCI

(b) Characteristics relevant to an investment in an associate are:

Significant influence over the activities of Archive.

Ownership of between 20% and 50% of the ordinary shares of archive.

Do not account for goodwill or recognise non-controlling interest as these are characteristics of accounting for a subsidiary where there is a relationship of control.

Workings

(W1) Group structure

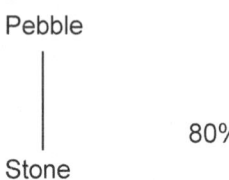

Pebble

80%

Stone

(W2) Net assets of Stone

	$ Reporting date	$ Acquisition	$ Post –acq
Share capital	60,000	60,000	
Share premium	10,000	10,000	
Retained earnings	250,000	150,000	
FV uplift ($180,000 – $150,000)	30,000	30,000	
	350,000	250,000	100,000

(W3) Goodwill

	$
Consideration	400,000
Add: NCI at acquisition	80,000
Less net assets at acquisition (W2)	(250,000)
	230,000

(W4) Non-controlling interest

	$
NCI at acquisition	80,000
NCI % of Stone post-acquisition retained earnings	20,000
(20% × $100,000 (W2))	
	100,000

(W5) Retained earnings

	$
100% of Pebble	295,000
PURP (W6)	(5,000)
80% of Stone post-acquisition retained earnings	80,000
(80% × $100,000 (W2))	
	370,000

(W6) PURP

Profit = $50,000 × 25% = $12,500

Profit remaining in group inventory = $12,500 × 2/5 = $5,000

The correcting entry is:

Dr Retained earnings (W5) $5,000

Cr Inventories (SOFP) $5,000

CHAPTER 21

1   B

	$	
Sales value	1,044	120%
Cost value	870	100%
Profit	174	20%

Workings:

Mark-up means profit is based on cost, therefore cost represents 100%. If profit is 20%, the sales value must be worth 120%.

Total profit is $174 and 60% is still in inventory = $104.40

2   A

	$000
S2m + ($1.5m× 3/12) – $0.1m	2,275

3   Answer

$10,300

	$000
10m + (4/12 × 6m)	12,000
Less: post-acq'n intra-group sales	(1,800)
Add: PURP re closing inventory	100
(1.8m × 20/120 × 1/3)	
	10,300

4   B

	$000
NCI share of group profit after tax	
(400 × 6/12 × 40%)	80

Note: Hopper made the intra-group sales and therefore bears all of the PURP adjustment. Only the post-acquisition element of Sooty's profit after tax is taken into account.

5   (a)   Goodwill on acquisition of Stockholm

		$000
Fair value of consideration paid		25,000
FV of NCI at acquisition		7,000
Less: net assets of S at acquisition:		
Issued equity capital	4,000	
Retained earnings at acquisition	20,000	
		(24,000)
Goodwill on acquisition		8,000

(b)

Consolidated statement of profit or loss for the year ended 31 December 20X6

	$000
Revenue ($200,000 + (6/12 × $100,000) – $12,500 inter-co))	237,500
Cost of sales ($110,000 + (6/12 × $50,000) – $12,500 inter-co + $1,000 PURP)	(123,500)
Gross profit	114,000
Distribution costs ($20,000 + (6/12 × $10,000))	(25,000)
Administrative expenses ($40,000 + (6/12 × $20,000))	(50,000)
Profit before tax	39,000
Income tax expense ($10,500 + (6/12 × $6,000))	(13,500)
Profit after tax	25,500
Profit attributable to:	
Owners of Pen (bal fig)	24,000
Non-controlling interest (W2)	1,500
	25,500

Refer to W1 for PURP

Refer to W2 for NCI

Workings

(W1) PURP and inter-company sales

Original cost plus 25% mark-up = $10m × 1.25 = $12,5m

This is the value of the inter-company sale and purchase which must be removed from both sales revenue and cost of sales.

Total profit on this sale = $12,5m – $10.0m = $2.5m

The proportion of this profit remaining in inventory must be eliminated:

40% × $2.5m = $1.0m

The double entry to adjust for this is:

Dr Cost of sales (P/L)	$1m
Cr Inventory (SFP)	$1m

(W2) Non-controlling interest

	$000
NCI % of (S's PAT – inter-co profit made by sub)	
(25% × ($7,000 – 1,000))	1,500

Index

Index

Index

Index